D1808082

Call Me Clyde

Call Me Clyde

Ann Johnson

Copyright © 2019 by Ann Johnson.

Library of Congress Control Number:		2019908327
ISBN:	Hardcover	978-1-7960-4223-8
	Softcover	978-1-7960-4222-1
	eBook	978-1-7960-4221-4

All rights reserved. No part of this book may be reproduced or transmitted in any form or by any means, electronic or mechanical, including photocopying, recording, or by any information storage and retrieval system, without permission in writing from the copyright owner.

Any people depicted in stock imagery provided by Getty Images are models, and such images are being used for illustrative purposes only.
Certain stock imagery © Getty Images.

Print information available on the last page.

Rev. date: 06/21/2019

To order additional copies of this book, contact:
Xlibris
1-888-795-4274
www.Xlibris.com
Orders@Xlibris.com
796885

I've been dead since September 5, 1985. Most people believe I'm dead and gone. The fact is, I'm only dead; I am not gone! The reason for this phenomenon is that I always relished each moment of life. Each moment was an adventure, a new story. Very few people have or had the lust for life that I did. Oh, hell, I've never known anyone quite like me. Neither have my friends or family. That's why I am writing this story. Or more appropriately, I'm going to let them tell the story, or at least the part fit to print.

Maybe I should tell you a little about myself first. That way you won't get confused later when others tell their stories. The most important thing that you should keep in mind is that I was one of the finest human beings ever to live. God endowed me with some great qualities: I was generous to a fault, had a fabulous sense of humor, hardworking with a keen sense of ethics, of high moral character—integrity was a hallmark of mine. (As I tell you all these things, I can only think of one fault that I did have. When I got embarrassed, I did clear my throat a bit.) I was loyal to my friends, loving to my wife and children, of which had six. Children, that is. I only had one wife: Ruthie, my bride.

I think we should start at the beginning so you will know what a remarkable fellow I truly was. I was born on August 14, 1918, at 11:00 in the morning. News just hit our little town of Walla Walla that the war had turned and it was only a matter of time. And not much time at that. The Second Battle of Marne had just turned back the Germans. They were retreating before the Allied counteroffensive. Everything looked good to us. August 14 was also destined to be the very day that the Japanese would surrender to end World War II in 1945 and that I would meet my wife.

This is only by way of introduction. For most of my life I was traveling salesman. I worked for Schick Blades and Razors. But in the beginning we carried pens and shampoo and anything else to grab our fair share of the market. To be a salesman in those days was a bit different than it is today. We would get into our cars on Monday morning and drag our asses home on Friday night. I had one of the biggest territories in Schick, Northern California, and most of Nevada, into Boise and parts of Oregon. Some weeks I was on the road two and three weeks before returning home. But you would run into other salesmen that made the job less lonely. I remember one night in Reno, a bunch of us went out to dinner. Now that's a salesman's dream. Harrah's Buffet. All you could eat. Marvelous stuff. Shrimp, crab, roast beef, and all the trimmings. But the best part was the price. In those days we got a per diem. So much money a day to eat with and sleep on. So if you were able to get a good meal for less than the daily allotment, you made money. And I had six kids at home to feed, along with my wife and her mother, Nellie. Now that's another story. Anyway, back to Reno. After dinner we would get together in one person's room and play cards. Actually we would play pinnacle. That was my favorite game because I always won. I taught the boys how to play myself. I was a *good* teacher.

Since Dad had worked for Warner–Lambert, I know he would enjoy going out in the field with me during the week. It would get him out of Mom's hair, and since most of the spiders in the neighborhood had fled in terror, it was the only responsible thing to do. I called Bob, my boss, who graciously acquiesced, stating, "Sure, Mary. It will do you good to get some professional tutoring, but don't tell John he's your father." John was a new rep at the time and assigned to work with me, learning to set up and price the shelves at a new Albertsons, and Bob didn't want John telling everyone in the company my dad was working with me.

I told Dad of Bob's seemingly simple restriction, which he accepted remarkably well. His quiet acceptance alone should have started alarm bells ringing. But being a trusting person, this subtle clue was lost on me. On the contrary, instead of any trepidation, I felt confident. No problems could or would occur. Dad could be a visiting manager from out of state, reviewing and critiquing our techniques, and as gullible as this new rep was, it was an easily believable story. Simple, straightforward, and with Dad's experience, an effortless, natural charade. Dad, of course, agreed, so early the next morning we left for the store.

I had agreed to meet John at the store by eight in the morning. Dad and I sat in the car for about fifteen minutes, waiting for John to arrive. Dad finally growled, "Why don't we get started? We can't wait for this asshole all day!" Turning my head to gaze at my patient father, I calmly replied, "Daddy, I'm supposed to train him. Just relax. We can get these racks set up quickly."

Changing the subject, Dad said, "Now how are we going to carry this thing off if you keep calling me Daddy. I'm your new boss. It's Clyde, remember."

"Okay, Clyde," I responded, returning to some reports.

About five minutes later, I heard this rumble next to me. "Well, I will just carry the racks in and look around."

What could I do? Resignedly, I gave up, saying "Okay, Daddy."

"Clyde!"

"Okay, Clyde."

We got the racks from the back of the car and carried them into the store. In the back of the store we found the stock we were to set up and price. Dad, I mean Clyde, reminded me at 9:30 that John still hadn't arrived. "The asshole still isn't here," he gravely informed me.

Answering contritely, "Yeah, you were right. It's a good thing we got started."

"That's okay, baby."

"Mary."

"Haha," he quietly laughed.

We had just finished the first rack about 10:00 when John finally made his long-awaited appearance. John walked up to me and explained that he had been held up because of a serious traffic accident ahead of him. Clyde turned back to his work, giving John a chance to cast his nervous glance first at me then at him, silently asking, "Who is this?"

"Mr. Preston," I interrupted Clyde, "This is John Seacrest, the new rep I'm training. John, this is Mr. Preston, a district manager from Northern California. He's here to review our display methods."

With a rather serious look, Clyde said, "That must have been a hell of a bad accident, but John, I've been with this company for over thirty years, and when an appointment is made, it's made."

John paled, apologized, and hurriedly began working.

Giving me a mischievous grin, Clyde said, "Mary, I think we can tell John the truth. The facts will be out soon enough anyway."

I looked at my father. The facts? What facts? What truth? That I am really his daughter? Somehow that didn't quite fit. Reluctantly, I replied, "Yes, Clyde."

"John," he said, "I'm really the new sales manager for this district. Bob has been dismissed. And call me Clyde."

Why not? His daughter does.

After about five very long minutes, John meekly asked, "Mr. Preston, what happened to Bob? Why was he dismissed?"

"Clyde!" Clyde chided. "John, what I tell you must not be discussed with anyone." John absorbed every word, knowing that something serious had happened. Daddy continued, "You see that asshole Bob was picked up for child molesting and is in jail right now. We don't know what will happen, but as of now, I'm your new boss."

John, stunned, mumbled, "Bob?"

"Yes. Isn't it a tragedy?"

My shock, different but no less intense than John's, caused me to move back a bit, away from the two of them. Feeling perhaps that token separation would help save my career.

Moments later, John, having regained some of his fleeting composure, inquired, "Clyde, ah, err, was it with his own children?"

Clyde slowly shook his head then solemnly informed John, "No, only with some of the neighborhood kids."

John was in shock, I'm sure, thinking of all the times that he and Bob had been alone together.

Finally, with a nasty laugh, Clyde mercifully tells John that he is my father and has retired from the company. John, still stunned and unsure, laughs a halfhearted laugh.

The three of us finished setting up and pricing the racks. Upon parting, Dad and I both told John not to mention this to anyone. It was just a joke.

That night after dinner, I received a call from Bob. He sternly asked, *"Why in the hell did you ever tell him I was a 'child molester'? Why couldn't you have told him I sold heroin or procured for women? Hell, anything but child molesting!"*

Well, needless to say, I was informed that my father was no longer welcome when training new reps.

And this was (is) just a part of the man I called Father.

Now isn't that a good story? Makes me laugh every time I think about it. You should have seen the look on John's face. Hell, you should have seen the look on my daughter's face! Mary actually staggered. We laughed all the way back to Mary's house. Clark, her husband (we'll get to him in a minute), and my bride (we'll get to her later too) just kept shaking their heads. They both knew full well it happened. Nothing ever surpassed my wife. She always said the same thing, in the same way, "*Oh, Clyde*!" For some reason she had to feign that she was shocked.

Now Clark. He's not at all like me. Much quieter. Matter of fact, most people are much quieter. I'm proud of the boy now. But wasn't always that way. He had to do some growing up first. Clark was in the service when he knocked my daughter up. That son of a bitch! I remember my life was shattered the day I found out my little girl was pregnant. My little girl thought she loved him. What could she know. And here it is thirty-two years later and they are still strolling along through life. And my little girl Mary, there is no dad prouder of his little girl than I am of her.

Clark has grown a lot from those first days. I remember one Sunday afternoon, part of the family went sailing in my rubber boat. Now *you* don't have to give me a bad time about my rubber boat. I took enough flack for that when I was alive. Yes, it was a boat, *not* a raft. It had a motor, and had to be named and licensed just like any other boat or yacht. I was very proud of my rubber boat. I got all the bells and whistles one could possible buy with a rubber boat. I even had a sail to go with it. Well, on this particular Sunday afternoon that I was talking about, there was a bit of a mishap. A boating accident. Actually, a sailing accident. My son-in-law was out on the water with my teenage son, Billy. I was on the shore with my bride, Ruthie, Mary, and Kym, her daughter. All of a sudden, from out of nowhere a big gust of wind blew up and capsized the boat. I have no idea what those assholes were doing out there. It took them an eternity to right the boat. They were much too far away for them to hear any instructions I could yell at them from shore. My daughter Mary was standing right beside me, mimicking everything I did. If I sighed, she sighed. If I stood, hands on hips, she stood, hands on hips. If I grunted, she grunted. If I paced, she paced. What in the hell were they doing out there anyway! Ruthie kept telling me it was all right. That was ridiculous. I could see everything wasn't all right. Clark and Billy had lost everything that was on board. I was standing there watching them try to recover all my new equipment. Finally, I jumped in the water, and Mary followed. We had to swim close to a half a mile to reach the scene. (Just a side note here, very few people can boast of being a better or faster swimmer than I was. I was always able to swim. I will tell you about that later, but Clark once said, "Dad had this strange modified stroke where he could carry a drink if need be, and probably swim forever." He was right; you never know when you need a drink. Swimming makes you awfully thirsty.) By the time we reached the boat, Clark was actually sweating. You can do that in water. It's a strange feeling. Clark had been working so hard. He was still intimidated by me, as most people were. He really was sweating. He had also recovered everything that was in the boat. Doesn't matter, I was still mad as hell. No consideration for other people's property. Well, we all got into the boat and went back to shore. *No one* said a word. Too scared. After we got back, we discovered one of the towels was missing. I asked as nicely as I could, "Where the hell is my goddamned towel?"

Clark replied, "I'll buy you another goddamned towel, Clyde!" That was the moment that Clark grew up! I was shocked as hell. The boy had it in him! I was proud of him. He was a man. I could trust that he could take care of my little girl. That is when Clark and I became peers.

You women don't know about things like this. You think you have all the answers, and you don't understand that men have a code. We live by this code. Men don't lie to one another, and our word is our bond, and we know what we have to do. One thing we have to do is to take care of our wives and families. We take great pride in our ability to care for our spouses. We men would lay down our lives for wives and children. I know we like our toys, but our greatest sense of pride comes from our ability to give you women every material comfort. This is our best means of expression. No, we don't talk a lot. Why should we? Remember actions speak louder than words! Now take my wife. I don't think she ever understood that, but a finer bride no man could ever have. Quite a woman, if I do say so myself.

I remember the day I met my bride. It was my birthday, August 14, 1945. Remember that day? Yes, it was a day for celebrating! Everyone around the world was whooping it up. WWII was over, Japan surrendered. Me and my buddy, McKnight Brunn, all dressed up in our navy uniforms, followed these two beautiful ladies into a liquor store in Alameda, California. We kinda mulled around while they made their purchase and followed them out. We asked, "Can we carry your packages home for you?" (Never hurts to be polite!) Lo and behold, they let us. Not only did they let us, but when we reminded them the only mannerly thing to do would be to invite us in for a drink, they did. Introducing ourselves, we found out these ladies were Mary Slatery and Ruth Irmen. We were batting a thousand when we were being ushered out of the little apartment. *Their boyfriends were coming over!* Can you imagine? Well, we left without tails tucked between our legs, but we still had to celebrate my birthday and the end of the war.

Everyone was celebrating; there was no lack of companionship. One of the best birthdays I ever had. I guess it was around 2:30 in the morning when I found myself knocking at Ruthie's door. No matter how much I knocked, she would not let me in. Finally she suggested that I come back when I was sober. Tail between my legs, I left again. Now you have to understand that I was not used to this abuse. Very rarely did I not get what I wanted with sheer animal magnetism. Have I mentioned that I was a very handsome guy besides all of my other unique qualities? Well, I was. Black hair came from my mother; she was half Cherokee. She was beautiful and soft and accomplished in all ways. She died when I was three.

Finally the next day I came back with chocolate and gum. Those items were very hard to find during and after the war. I had her hooked. The rest, as they say, is history. We got married eight months later, on May 7, 1946. I will get back to my wife in a minute, but I must first tell you about McKnight Brunn. I got to know him in the service. As I said, we were buddies. After the war was over, he went back to being a lawyer. He took care of all my legal affairs, wills and such. Had to keep revising it after each kid. You know I had six of them. Well, Mac, as we all called him, was a very intelligent guy. I'm sure you can imagine, being a lawyer and all. But to tell you the truth, dumb as a box of rocks. Do you know what I mean? Had to take care of him. Without me, he was lost. He, of course, knew that better than me. So I am going to let him tell you a bit of those war days.

When I first met Press, that was my name for him, I was with Pan American Airways and was just transferred to Ile Nou, a small island in the bay at Noumea, New Caledonia, where Press was serving as a petty officer in the Naval Air Transport Service of which the Pan American Airways operations were a part. We were there for more than a year, as I recall, and each day was a story in itself, and it would take forever to try to tell them all. I returned to San Francisco sometime in 1943, as I recall, and was mustered into the navy as a petty officer myself. Then I was transferred to Pearl Harbor for duty with the Naval Air Transport Service. Our barracks were in an old auditorium, which had all of the seats and stage torn out and replaced by a wooden floor and totally covered by double bunks in groups of four, jammed up against each other, being separated by the next group by an aisle about two feet wide. We had no lockers. The only lavatory facilities were the auditorium complex itself. They were outside and down the steps into the basement. They consisted of two toilets, two urinals, and two wash basins for all five hundred of us. On about the fifth day after my arrival, while I was sitting on my bunk, pondering this ridiculous situation, I heard Press' jovial and inimitable voice saying, "Hey, Mac, get your stuff and come with me!"

Press had been transferred to Pearl Harbor from Noumea sometime before, and I don't know how he found out I was there. But it did not take me long to get my stuff together, because my duffel bag had been lost, and all I had was the clothing I was wearing. The sight and sound of Press were mighty welcome.

I followed him for half a mile, or so, over to the engine overhaul sheds right next to the ocean where we found spare upper bunk, not far from the head. We were surrounded by engine mechanics and equipment of all types. Press had a nearby bunk. In the bay, through the door, the special planes, for such people as Admiral Tower, were under repair. With Press' help, I borrowed a three-star blanket from Admiral Tower's PBM, which I used for the rest of the time I was in Hawaii. During all the time after that, I enjoyed the companionship of Press who always had a running pinochle game (at which he was always a perennial winner). He always knew where we could get a drink when we felt the need for one, and he always *excelled* as a scrounger for anything and everything.

If it was possible for me to enjoy life during those days, I believe it was Press that made it so. Enjoying life was not always easy. For example, twenty-four hour of every day, at least six aircraft engines, on test stands, were operating full tilt within twenty-four feet of our bunks. I don't see how we were able to talk. And I don't see how we got out of there still able to hear.

From that time on we were transferred, first to Oakland Naval Air Station, where he met his wife, then to Oletha Naval Air Station in Kansas. No matter where we were, Press managed to find "outside" activities. Often he failed to show up at muster on time or at all, and I regularly answered for him at roll call; I don't believe he was ever found out.

Press and I were as different as night and day, but Press and his great laugh, good humor, generosity, and friendship were my salvation during all those weird navy days. I will never forget him.

Now didn't I tell you about Mac? And those were his own words. He was right about one thing: Every day was a different story. I remember one party that we went to, actually crashed. It was full of Hollywood starlets. Mac forgot to mention that part of my job during those years was to fly with the USO from one destination to another. Take care of them; babysit them. Because I could improvise, I was considered by my superiors to be one of the best at my job. And they didn't want to know how I got the job done; they only wanted to know that I got it done. And I never disappointed them. Matter of fact, I can't recall anyone I ever did disappoint. Well, this one night, Barbara Stanwick was hosting a little gathering before she took off for New Caledonia. Well, I thought it only neighborly of me to introduce myself to her, seeing as how I was to be her escort. She was in a gay mood and was delighted that I would be so kind as to put myself out before I actually had to. I told her that "putting myself out" for others just came naturally to me. Well, Mac and I were in, and the party was swinging. After we found our way to the bar, we started making the rounds. I was a pro at this. It wasn't long before Mac and I split up. You can cover more ground that way. Now Mac needed excitement but not as much as I had in mind. Now there was one little girl there that struck my fancy. She was small with dark hair and a dark dress on with a big white collar. Now as far as I could tell, she was having a fine time, mighta' fine. And she seemed to be particularly fond of an army fellow. But I knew the way to get her attention. I snuggled right up to her and slowly put my hand on her knee. Then slowly, ever slowly, started up her dress, passed the top of her nylons, and almost to the bottom of her panties before *crash*. Her hand came down and she started to scream, "What are you doing?"

"Just trying to make an impression," I told her.

"Well, you sure as hell did that! Couldn't you make an impression another way?" she asked.

"I probably could," I said, "but this one will last a lifetime, I haven't found any other way that will do that." With that she and all around started to laugh. I was the belle of the ball again.

Women wanted me, and I know it. Just one of those things. In the air transport, we had our own newspaper called *Nats and Bolts*. One of my buddies put a joke in it that kinda suited me:

Chief Preston: "What's that book your reading?"

Warrant Officer Polak: "It's entitled, 'What twenty million women want.'"

Chief Preston: "Yeah? Let's see if they spelled my name correctly!"

That kinda sums it up. But that all changed the day I met my bride. Ruthie was a beautiful woman. (However, I never met an ugly one. That's the truth!) But Ruthie, she was different. Maybe because she was Catholic, or maybe her upbringing, or maybe it was just her, but she was special. In all the years we were married, I never fell out of love with her; she was always my bride. Ruthie was soft and kind, and the most capable woman I ever met. Rarely did she complain, and was quick to smile. She was my most wonderful lover and closest friend. We shared on the deepest level that anyone could ever imagine. I think she could read my mind. She always amazed me. Not only could she make the most wonderful meals, and with such variety (remember the household was rather large), but she had this unique ability to completely and efficiently run the house while I was gone and then when I would emerge on Friday night, turn me back into the king of the castle. I've talked to other men that don't even travel, and they feel like strangers in their own home. They feel their wives make all the decisions and they have to ask permission to sit at the table for dinner. But not Ruthie. The moment that I got home from a trip, she somehow turned the decision making over to me. Not that she wasn't just as capable when I was home—she was, but she made me head of the house. The kids had to come to me and check the family plans, and ask me permission to go with their friends and such.

That was only one unique thing about her. Maybe the very best thing was that she and I were a perfect match. We complemented each other, we fed off each other, and we fed each other. Not that we didn't have our ups and downs—we did! The stories that I could tell you, the stories I will tell you. Now you already know that we got married eight months after the war ended. But what you don't know is that I went back to United Airlines. I had worked for them before the war started as a passenger agent. So when Ruthie and I got married, I had a job right there in San Francisco waiting for me. Our first home was in Brisbane, a little suburb close to the airport. One night Don Ameche came in while I was in the back. The other passenger agent that I was working with that shift called me out to wait on him, saying he was busy. As I waited on Don, he looked straight into my eyes and said, "It's rather strange to look at a complete stranger, and feel that you're looking in a mirror!" He was right. I had that same weird feeling looking at him. People had said we looked alike, and they were right. This was the first and only time I met him. But that's not the story I was going to tell you.

After Ruthie and I got married, I was anxious to show her off to all of my friends. I had worked in San Francisco before the war, so I know a lot of people. Ruthie had come to work in Alameda, to help in the war effort, from her hometown in Bisbee, North Dakota. Now one fellow that I knew back then was Johnny De Marco. A character if you ever met one. Ruthie always referred to him as my "gangster buddy." Johnny was the proprietor of a friendly little gambling joint in Brisbane. Yes, you had to know someone to get in to the private part of the club. My bride was more than a little skeptical the first time I took her to his establishment. Although anyone could go into the dance hall on the main floor, only special people could go upstairs. Ruthie said it made her nervous to be peered at through a peephole in a door as if *she* were the strange one. The secret password was something she was not used to, and she clung to me as if I were a life boat. I didn't mind! My good friend Johnny knew how to make *most* people feel at home.

Offering drinks and *anything* else that would help a guy relax after a hard day's, or night's, work. Johnny wasn't married then, but his future wife worked for him at this time. She was in charge of those gracious ladies that know just how to help a man "take his mind off his work." What an operation. He had a gold mine. And San Francisco was rather accommodating in those days. Sally Stanford ran her establishment out of San Francisco. Later she would move, or be moved to Sausalito, just north of the Golden Gate, and Johnny down here. But Johnny had the edge with the gambling. I think what made my bride the most nervous was Johnny's eyes. She informed me, "His eyes keep moving. He never really looks at you, always watching everything. I think something is about to happen any minute." But we were as safe at DeMarco's as a babe in their mother's arms. For you see, Johnny had a special relationship with our noble law enforcement. And my bride was to learn to marvel at this man who was barely taller than the 5'2" that she stood. Come to think of it, not even Mr. J. Russell Spencer, of 20th century Fox, could have cast or directed a more perfect actor in Johnny's role.

One day one of my buddies came to me with a rather large problem. He had been picked up for drunk driving. They didn't use *driving while under the influence* then. They called it what it was. He was going to lose his license for sure. So I went to my old "gangster buddy," as my bride called him, to see if Johnny could do anything. (My bride was right; his eyes moved all the time.) He would see what he could do. Well, my friend—nameless for the purpose of this story, as I'm sure you can understand why—appeared before the court on his appointed day. He had no lawyer; he trusted me. Most people trust me. When the court clerk called his name, he stood up and went to the front of the room. The judge said, "Are you_____?" And my friend replied, "Yes, Your Honor." (Never hurts to be polite.) The judge pronounced, "Case dismissed!" Did we celebrate that night! But we never let that guy ever drive again when drinking.

Few people ever know about my deep religious nature. Deep, however, depends on what yardstick is used. It burns my ass that some ultra-religious bastard counts me as damned. The fact is God and I understand (always had an understanding). After all, I was baptized. My baptismal certificate reads, "This certifies that in obedience to the command and in imitation of the example of our Lord Jesus Christ, Clyde E. Preston was buried with him in baptism" on the 28th day of April 1929 at Newport, Oregon. G. W. Gay by Mildred L. Edwards, Clark.

Believe me, I was ten and a half years old and fully knew my mind. The Pacific waters were cold as hell the day they dunked my head under the water and I emerged a member of the First Christian Church. Son of a bitch, there had to be a better way. Years later when I married my Catholic wife, I found they had a more humane way of performing the same ritual.

Speaking of my bride, she seemed to get me to church every time I turned around. There were all those baptisms, holy communions, confirmations, and weddings for six kids. Beside all those special occasions I even submitted myself to Christmas and Easter until the kids were a little older. The good Lord knows I did my part. I even started saying grace at family meals after thirty years of marriage.

Now there was one woman in particular who could see me, right down to the depth of my inner soul. That was Elizabeth, my bride's sister. Truthfully, folks, I'm not sure if I want her to speak. I know she will embarrass the hell out of me. Yet she has asked. I am sure as shit I can't stop her.

My first introduction to Clyde was in a letter. I began to know Clyde a few years before we met. I remember the first letter Ruth wrote to me about him. It was when and how they met. She was living in Alameda in August of 1944. My sister and her roommate were planning cocktails for their boyfriends. Before going out, they decided to splurge and get a nice bottle of bourbon. Because it was wartime, it was a real luxury. My sister and Mary Slattery walked to a liquor store. They were followed by two young navy men. Clyde walked up to Ruthie and asked if he could carry their bags home; they agreed. When they reached the apartment, Ruthie invited the men in for a drink. They had one drink then were ushered out. Their boyfriends were coming. After midnight, Clyde came knocking on the door. My sister wouldn't let him in, so Clyde came back the next day. And it all started. Ruthie knew from the start that Clyde was different, much different. They were married just less than eight months later.

Every week my sister wrote me a new story. Yet the story I want to tell started late summer of 1963. I had been quite ill. None of the doctors in North Dakota knew what was wrong. Ruthie could no longer stand by and see me suffer. She told Clyde. The next thing I knew everything was arranged. Myself and four of my nine children traveled out west. We were to stay with them, get the kids in school, and wait for my husband and three more of my children to join us. They had to sell the house, finish the house painting, and tie up loose ends.

The train ride was extremely hard on me. I was thoroughly exhausted and sick to my very marrow when I reached their home.

I will never be able to tell you the feelings—warmth, security, and peace—I felt as I walked through that door. Ruthie had been busy, all right. Her whole house was rearranged even before we arrived there. Before we arrived, there were nine people living in their five-bedroom home. Now there were to be fourteen. It was Ruthie that did all the cooking, cleaning, and washing. I was too ill to help. It was Ruthie that shopped, chauffeured kids, and kept the household running as perfectly as a well-oiled machine. But it was Clyde that paid for it all. And we women know, especially in the early 1960s, who was king of the castle.

That isn't to take away from Clyde, not one bit. That was a sign of the times; we had been raised that way. It was Clyde's compassion and generosity. It was Clyde's love for his wife; it was Clyde's soul that brought us here! His generosity didn't stop at paying our way out or keeping us in his home. It continued just before my husband Walter arrived. He rented a house for us and brought us furniture. After my husband got to Rancho Cordova, Clyde got him a job at Aerojet. For the first time in his life, he was making good money. I had never seen my husband boast as proud as a peacock. But he did now. For this was the first time in his life he made enough money to pay taxes.

You would think Clyde's heart good as gold; even if I stopped the story here, yet, there's more to tell. After Walter was settled in his job, Clyde and, of course, my sister (remember it's still the early sixties) put down a payment on a home for us, co-signed our loan, and bought us more furniture. Yet this still isn't the end. After I died of a brain tumor (they finally found out why I had suffered so terribly those eight years) and my husband's death of leukemia two years after mine, Clyde and my dear sister wanted to take my two little ones, Nellie and Matt, to live with them to raise them, to keep and cherish them.

Yet God decided and, I concurred, a different life for my babies. But that doesn't change the fact that Clyde's heart was as true as God's stars, and as pure as his heavens his soul. Clyde is now with us in heaven and believe me, we are all a bit livelier. It was a shock to know he made a stop in purgatory. No matter how short it was. I knew him and felt his presence. I read his soul. He was generous and humble. Humility is truth, exemplified truth. He was true to himself. He was true to his beliefs. And what's more, he was true to the gifts God gave him. There were only a few people that saw Clyde as I did. Many expected him to be in purgatory for half of eternity. But no person who knew Clyde expected him to end up in hell. I hope I can speak again, because even though I have told the truth, the whole truth and nothing but the truth, we must face the fact that Clyde was a man. Therefore he could be a real asshole. Yet, now is not the time to speak of that.

Before I turn these pages back to Clyde, I want to introduce you to another who knows Clyde's spiritual worth. His name is Monsignor Richard Dwyer. Yet when I belonged to his parish, it was Fr. Dwyer. He is a living saint. By the way, the definition of a saint is one who does God's will. Monsignor Dwyer always held Clyde in the deepest respect. Clyde never had a higher respect for any living creature. It might have been that they shared the same birthdays and retired on the same day that held them in close bonds. Whatever the reason, they were two souls who met and touched on earth. There is at least one other thing they shared. That was a total respect for others. They, like most men, respected the views they held in common, but these two men, along with a few others, also respected a man's views that differed from theirs, if and only if that person was true to themselves, given that person's circumstances. In other words, they both expected people to grow but tried not to squash that growth. Only encourage it. Without further ado, as they say, here is Monsignor Richard Dwyer.

My dear Elizabeth, thank you for your most kind words of both about me and Clyde. Yet I would like to disagree for a moment. You recognized Clyde because of your own inherent goodness. I remember presiding over your funeral mass. It was the first time I cried in public. The release of your soul from this earth was also the release of mine. I have only recently found out the reason for this suffering.

It seems that it was quite some time before I felt that suffering in you (knew you were suffering at all). You, Elisabeth, opened the door. Your life let me see the suffering of others on all levels. Suffered the agony of poverty, some physically, others emotionally, psychologically, or spiritually. Even though I dealt with all of these before, I now saw them in a new light. Clyde dealt with them also. His approach, however, was "hands-on." Maybe the best secular way of dealing with it? I never knew him to turn away from someone in need. He wasn't a professional, and many times he didn't know what to say, yet he always did the right thing.

But what I remember most about Clyde was that he was generous to a fault even if he did not know the person. He had a great sense of humor. When anyone was with Clyde, they knew they were in the presence of greatness. He was the most remarkable person I have ever met. Truly I am so happy I got to know him. I have never seen the love he had for people and life—just amazing.

Clyde—with the question in his eyes and heart one day while sitting in my office, here was a man, a good and honest man, who married a

Catholic girl twenty-five years before. This man had sacrificed many things to send his kids to parochial school. A school that was to teach true Christian virtue, and yet, his children turned out no different than any others in the late sixties. I knew how much he loved Ruthie to not only be married in the church but to raise their children Catholic. I knew his deep conviction of Christianity. I knew how devoted he was to his children and their need for special upbringing. Yet he was not Catholic though it mattered little to me. How could I explain to him, this pure heart, the Catholic church had seemingly failed. I had failed. For some reason Clyde always held me in the highest esteem. Elizabeth, thank you again for letting me speak.

My husband truly was the most wonderful man. He loved me beyond what anyone could imagine, but everyone saw it with their own eyes. It couldn't be missed. How he learned to love with such greatness is beyond me. His brother did not turn out at all like him, but his sister did.

When Clyde was out of town, he would call every night, He would ask me about my day and how our children were, usually starting with the youngest, and to make sure I was doing fine, and tell me about his day. There were always stories to tell. He kept me and everyone else entertained. He was not afraid to tell me anything. Over time, his buddies sent a lady of the night to his room. I knew Clyde would never cheat on me even if he were gone for three weeks.

My dad was a traveling salesman for the Schick Safety Razor Co. and later taken over by Warner–Lambert. Being a traveling salesman meant our dad was not home every night. As a matter of fact, I think he was probably gone more often than not.

Sometimes when my dad returned from his out-of-town trips, he would bring us gifts. They weren't expensive and he did not always bring them. I remember running out to the car to greet my daddy, anxious to see what awesome gift he had brought. The one gift that sticks out was a pair of those dark paper sunglasses, the kind you get after an eye exam.

Now that I write this, I realize that he must have recently been to the eye doctor. As a young child you don't see the weakness of your parents, and he certainly never complained of any problems in front of his children. He let me know that those were my special gift and I love them.

My dad looked like Don Amechi who at the time when we were youngsters had a circus show on TV, *The Big Top* (I think). So on those nights our dad was not home, we got to see him on TV. Somewhere deep inside, I knew it was not my dad, but I just went with the enchantment that that was my daddy on TV.

When I was about four or five, he took us girls on one of his Reno trips. My dad handed me the keys to open the motel door. Oh, how excited I was to open a door with a key! It would have been a first for me. Just as I was about to put the key into the keyhole, a man walked up, took the key from me, and said, "Let me open the door for the daughter of Don Amechi." Well, I was proud to be the daughter of such a famous person, but I really wanted to open that door all by myself.

Almost every summer our dad would take us camping, and as far back as I can remember, he always set up a golfing area. He was a great golfer; he loved to golf and had many trophies for his hole in ones. He was also a skilled pinochle player. Our mom didn't understand why his card buddies would come back week after week to lose their hard-earned money to our dad, but they did. My dad said that is how he paid for his girls' weddings.

There are always fond memories, or should I say warm happy feelings, while feasting during the holidays. Mom, Dad, Grandmother, and six kids only make nine, but bring my cousins and a few friends to the table and that meant food for at least twenty-two. That was a normal number for our holiday dinners. We kids all had duties to perform, *not* in the traditional way you may think. One duty was if you walked into the kitchen, and a pot was cooking on the stove, you stirred it. Every kid in my family knows that one. Another was to greet the guests and offer to take their coats/hats and or purse and lay it neatly on my mom and dad's bed. Set the table the day before if possible, after the dusting and vacuuming were done and in between cooking anything that could be precooked and fixing hors d'oeuvres. Usually Janine and I would get up to clear dishes after people had finished eating and sit back down for a smoke and a drink of Grand Marnier (when we were old enough). It wasn't too rough, but these chores were performed by the girls only; you know, I don't think the boys even had to clean their own bedrooms. I am just saying! Actually the boys missed out on a lot of camaraderie.

During dinner, with all the people, the noise level was abuzz. I have images of people taking good healthy bites of delicious-looking food and chattering all about. My dad would sit at the head of the table looking at his lovely bride, "Ruthie Baby," at the other end with their children scattered among the crowd. My dad was a proud man, proud of his family and proud of his accomplishments and justly so being able to feed all of us. I never thought about how expensive those grocery bills could have been, until just now.

To change the subject just a little, there is this picture of my dad between Ann and Janine as they are kissing him on the cheek. He had just been given a medal, after a dinner party in his honor, by Senator Matsu for his bravery in saving a drowning man. You can just see how proud he was at that moment to have received such a prestigious award and having two of his beautiful daughters supporting him at his side.

Our dad was a lucky man, lucky at keno, lucky with raffles. He was always winning something. He won his trips to Mexico, but that is because he worked hard for those trips. Mexico was a favorite place for our mom and dad. My dad loved to walk along the beach and collect shells. Later he would make beautiful picture frames or frames for mirrors. He made a beautiful bathroom set for our mom.

His luck was also good when it came to getting out of traffic tickets. I heard tales of him walking the police officer to the back of his car to the trunk where his samples were stored. My dad had a gift to sell, and the next thing you know, he and the officer are buddies. Our dad drives away without a ticket, and the officer is now a Schick safety razor man with an arm full of great merchandize.

Our dad took the RV trailer to our cousin's wedding in Los Angeles. The next morning, very early, he was ready to get back home. He was a little anxious sometimes. He got pulled over for a taillight being out. Well, he had three of his kids asleep in the back of the trailer, which was against the law. Not that we always drove back there, but if we did, we were told not to open the door unless we heard my dad knock. This police officer was a-knocking and a-knocking, but there was no response from inside. Our mother was thankful we were all passed out from celebrating the night before.

People loved coming over to our home, and it was a home, not a house. We were all welcoming except my mother. Now that's another story that we won't go into. I really want them to tell their stories.

Because of Clyde's and my tremendous love for each other, the kids grew up knowing how to love. Each of them has a unique story. The first home the kids lived in was in Redwood City. Back in the old days, people were very much nicer. We had some great neighbors in a great safe neighborhood. The kids could go out to play. We required them to be three or older. Younger need a grown-up to be with them. One of our next-door neighbors had three kids. Jackie, a teenager, and her brother, Sonny, was thirteen and also Pidge, the youngest, was eleven. Jackie would babysit when my bride and I would go out. One day close to Halloween, my daughter, Ann, who was three years old, asked Pidge what he was doing and he said, "Making a mask to scare you." She said, "Now that I know it, you can't scare me." A few days later, Ruthie and I went out for a nice dinner, and Jackie was the babysitter. It was that night that Pidge went into our backyard. Our picket fence was very short, and we had gate between our homes. The kids were all asleep; we had three in the same large room with a window between each of the three beds. The home was old and the windows were only two feet off the floor. So Pidge went to the window between Ann and Mary's bed. He tapped on the window and woke Ann up. She screamed bloody murder and woke the others. They all ran into the front room where Jackie was, and she tried everything to calm down the kids, especially Ann. She was the only one that saw the mask. Jackie finally decided to make some peanut butter and jelly sandwiches; we did not have enough jelly. So Jackie went to her home to get some. That's when my bride and I got home. We truly freaked out when Jackie came back in. I must confess I was calm and asked, "Where have you been?" I did not have to ask how long she had been gone when her answer was, "My brother scared Ann, and Mr. Preston and I did everything I could think of to calm her down. So I decided to make PB&J to calm her down and you did not have enough jelly, so I went and got some, see?" That was not the last time she babysat for us.

I must say, I am enjoying this book and the stories that are told by others. But now I am taking over.

Every year my bride and I would go somewhere wonderful on a summer trip. We were always gone over the Fourth of July. Schick would give me two weeks off. I made an amazing amount of money, but living through the Depression and WWII, my bride and I would save a considerable amount. This turned out to be a very good thing because when I retired, we were well taken care of. When we were younger, we would visit family. One year we would go to Ruthie's family to visit, and the next we would visit my family. The kids would always like to go to my mom and dad's ranch. Well, actually, my dad's and his wife. She was not my mother. My mother, Anna, was one-half Cherokee and one-half Scottish. She died giving birth to my youngest brother. I was the second boy. For several years we guys ran the ranch. We had a large ranch—wheat, vegetable garden, horses, and cows. This is where I learned to work hard. Being a farmer and going to school did not give me much time to do anything else

The kids helped get bales of hay onto the flatbed that was pulled behind the tractor. Then the bales had to be stacked. That was a lot of hard work. Gardening was more fun, especially gathering the fruits and vegetables for dinner. And the food we ate was much different than what my bride cooks.

It was the first time the kids used an outhouse. We would also visit my sister and her family. They lived close. They had a much bigger home and ranch. Phyllis and Tom only raised wheat. Also the kids had more fun with their three kids and all the horses they had. Everyone got to ride their own horse. Sleeping was more comfortable. Their three kids were about the same age as ours.

Phyllis was one child of Velma and my dad George had, and I was ten years older than her. Ruthie liked it best there too. There was not a lot of work there because Tom had hired hands. They also drank and Ruthie enjoyed two Tom Collins at night, relaxing after a busy day with the kids. We also played family games with the kids. So going to Washington was oh, so much fun for everyone.

When we would go to Ruthie's side, mostly in North Dakota, the kids love going to her sister Elizabeth and Walter's home, nine kids. A house with three floors, and Ann loved going into the basement and looking at all the treasures, but was sure there was a ghost down there so she would not go down by herself. She also like the second oldest girl Kathryn, she took care of the kids, kept them out of we parents hair. She would also tell the most fun stories. We would also visit Veta and her brother. Both of them had more money than Elizabeth. Sigrid, Irmen, Kathryn, Frank, Jack, Anne, Tony, Matt, Nellie. But Elizabeth was the best. We would eventually have them live with us while Walter sold the house and leave his job. When my wife found out her sister had major medical problems, she wanted me to help her. I would do anything for my wonderful bride. So we bought the train tickets for her and the four youngest kids so they could get ready for school. They lived with us for about six months until Walter could come out. We helped them buy a house and found Walter a job. I was always able to get whatever anyone needed. I am truly a remarkable man.

One year we went to the Royal Gorge. We camped as we did many places. There is so much to do and see, and it's quite a learning place. Everyone loved the train ride and all the conductor would say about all we saw. The old West town was very informative. The kids like the history of where we came from. Both my bride's and my family were in the U.S. since the 1700s. We went gold panning for the first time and all got a bit of gold by my daughter Mary. She was so upset. We did not go river rafting because we had two very young ones. We did go camping a lot especially at Big Sur. That is on the ocean. While there you must keep our food in a kotch in the trees or the wild boar will get into it. That's not good. They would visit usually at night but don't harm people. Going to the ocean, there is plenty to see and we camped close to shore. The kids and Ruthie would pick up shells for souvenirs and look at all the amazing shape of the coast that the water would make by erosion. Monterey also had big clams that you could eat. Each year we would also go to Half Moon Bay to go smelting. That where you catch wonderful small fish. The female smelt would get on the shore and lay their eggs. You need a big-shaped net that at least two people hold and once the fish swim in, you scoop up the net, collecting the fish. At that point, you go farther up the sand and empty the net for the rest of the family to pick up and put into bags. They taste great, especially the way Ruthie would cook them. She was a fantastic cook. Did I tell you that before? When the kids were older, we would go to Mexico, usually the Baja. We went there so many times we made friends with the locals.

We were also invited to one for dinner and later invited to their daughter's wedding and we went. I also saved a man's life down there. The man was older than me and was swept out by the waves. I jumped into the ocean, swam out, and saved him I was a very strong swimmer, both me and my brother Earl. We learned to swim when we were very young. Either he or I would always win the races. When I reached the guy, he was under the water and I had to give him mouth-to-mouth right there before I had him back to shore. This was the fifth life I saved. My older son, Tom, and oldest daughter, Ann, and grandson Paul have saved lives. It runs in the family. We always stayed on the water and the first time I tasted turtle, oh so good. We would go clamming and I would serve those clams in many ways. Normally I would cook breakfast because I was the first one up. Have you ever had clam pancakes? And of course, we would have them in the traditional way too. The waters down there are much calmer. We also had a fifth wheeler so when we parked, we could unhook the truck and go anywhere much faster. Getting that was much cheaper than going to hotels all the time.

I have always loved the ocean! Sitting quietly forever watching the waves break time after time in endless motion. Here was the only place I could sit motionless, happy to let the ocean move for us both. Only the ocean quiets the body while energizing the soul. Here you become one with nature and God.

Depending on the time of year, we would do something fun. During the summer we would go hiking, fishing, boating, and swimming in the pool or Folsom Lake, which was closer than the ocean. We all liked to swim. I only told you about three men. I saved six altogether. The first was when I was eighteen years old at the Pacific coast of Oregon. Same type of scenario. A younger guy was being swept out by a strong tide. He did not know to swim parallel to the shore till the tide was not so strong. Again I jumped into the water and reached him as he was going under, exhausted by his battle with the water. Had I not reached him when I did, he would have gone under. My dad taught my brother Earl and I how to swim. Whenever we were in a race, either he or I would win. Always!

Winters were more inside. We liked to play all sorts of games. One my bride invented was Dictionary. It was a way to help the kids learn much more. Each person would take one of the dictionaries—we had three. Big family. They'd look up a word and write down the definition. We usually picked out three words and we hoped that the other players would not know the word like Kwa Zulu. When it was our turn, we would say the word and spell it. Everyone else would write down the word on the small pieces of paper and make up a definition, if they did not know the word. Then the word giver would collect all the pieces of paper and read them to his or herself. If they had a question, they would take the person into the other room and ask the question. Each person also wrote their name on the paper. Than the presenter would read all of the definitions and each got to choose the one they thought was the best. If you choose the correct one, you would get a point. The person that got the most points won. Charades was also a good one, bouncing around the room. Everyone love to be the one standing up in our large living room preforming. We also had Monopoly and other board games.

I am Linda the fourth kid, and now it is my turn. Here are some of my memories. Once on a trip to Mexico with my parents, a Mexican came strolling into our camp at Club de Pesc in San Felipe. This man was selling these beautiful cotton shirts with colorful flowers embroidered around the neckline. I don't remember how much the man was asking for these shirts, maybe $10.00 each. Well, my dad wanted to get three— one for my mom and one for my sister and myself. So, of course, the haggling began. You could see that my dad and this man, we found out later to be Mr. Guzman, were both enjoying the bantering back and forth.

Finally my dad said to him, "Hell, I got this shirt back in the states for only $1." Mr. Guzman did not hesitate. He pulled a dollar bill out of his pocket and gestured for my dad's shirt, and stuffed the dollar bill into my father's hand. At this point my dad knew he had said the wrong thing, but all he could do was to giggle. Yes, my dad giggled, and Mr. Guzman proceeded to unbutton my father's shirt. My dad could not stop giggling while Mr. Guzman undressed him. Literally took the shirt right off my father's back. My dad's girls got their shirts, Mr. Guzman got his shirt, and my dad got an American dollar bill and a friend for life. My father invited him for dinner and told him to bring his family. My dad liked to feed and entertain people. Luckily we had just purchased these big, tasty-looking shrimp. As my mom and I began to butterfly the shrimp to be breaded, we looked out the little RV kitchen window to see the Guzmans arriving. There must have been twelve in the party. Good thing we had an extra bag of shrimp and were able to feed them all.

One thing my father always did was to encourage his guest to eat more. "Have some more," he would say, even after their second helping. Our parents made sure there was always plenty of food. We were very fortunate not to be deprived of anything. Our father was a hardworking man, a traveling salesman. I remember hearing more than once, "Your dad could sell an ice cube to a penguin." (At that time, there was no fear of losing our glaciers, so selling ice to a penguin really would be an achievement.) The point is, our dad was a very good salesman; he won many prizes through his company for being top salesman, some of which were trips—trips to Mexico City and the Yucatan. My mom loved them. She loved Mexico and my dad did so want to please her, and of course he did many times. He would refer to her as his lovely bride, Ruthie Baby. Maybe through the trips he won, they both realized they had a love for Mexico.

So back to our San Felipe story. One good turn deserves another, so the Guzmans invited us to their house for dinner. They served ceviche, a first for all of us. Raw shrimp, but we ate and enjoyed it. Conversations were a little difficult, but we managed with our limited knowledge of the Spanish language and hand gestures. After dinner my dad decides he wants to tell a joke. It was my mom and me that knew some Spanish. My dad did not know any, but he figures he'll be able to tell it because it is a visual joke. So he grabs one of the cloth napkins and starts talking while he's folding this napkin. Everyone is listening intently, not really knowing what my dad is saying. Then all of a sudden this napkin turns into what looks like a throbbing penis and my dad says, "Now isn't that a peach," and everyone started to laugh. Maybe it was because my dad was so tickled with himself and was giggling so contagiously that everyone laughed.

As us kids were growing up, the holidays were the best! Our mother and grandmother always decorated the house and had us help. The living room became Christmas. They would take all the regular knick-knacks off the coffee table, the end tables, and fireplace and replace them with the nativity, angels, candles, and an apple turned into a Santa. (I loved the Apple Santa that our grandmother would create each year; it was so cute.)

What made this truly a magical wonderland was early on Christmas morning, we were allowed to enter the room one at a time only after our dad was set up to film us. (Back in the day, it wasn't called a video; it was a moving picture show.) This camera had four highly intense bright lights attached to it and aimed right into our sleepy little eyes. After the blinding light, seeing the living room with everything lit up, sparkling, and shining, we knew there was no doubt that Santa had been to visit our home.

I am Tom and am back. As you know, Dad traveled all the time as a salesman with Schick, and Nellie, Mom's mom, stayed at our home and Mom and Dad had a very large picture of a Polynesian girl dancing scantily dressed and it was framed with a glass cover. When he was gone, she would use fingernail polish and cover her up with a dress. When he returned home from one of his trips, he found that the Polynesian girl had a dress. It seems that Nellie (whom he referred to her as "old lady") had used fingernail polish and had painted a dress on the dancer. Dad said nothing, but that night, removed the nail polish. On Dad's next trip, the dress reappeared. I think that this happened three or four times before Grandmother stopped covering her in nail polish. It seemed as if they were like oil and water, but they were more alike than not. On one of Dad's trips, he was going to Oregon, and he took the "old lady" with him as Nellie's brother lived somewhere in Oregon. On the trip, Dad asked, "Old lady, have you ever been over 100 miles per hour?" (Footnote: Nellie got a driver's license in the mail and drove a car through town and supposedly got a ticket for exceeding 15 miles per hour.) Well, back to Dad, who wasn't a slow driver. He got the car up over a hundred miles per hour and got pulled over by an Oregon policeman. Dad was the nicest, as a good salesman can be, and got a ticket for going over 80 miles per hour. After the ticket had been written, Dad told the officer he was a salesman and he "wasn't" trying to change anything, but part of his job was to hand out free samples to get people interested in the newest Schick product. He then asked the officer where he could go to pay the ticket. The officer told him the next town had a gas station and the owner was the local justice of the peace. So Dad got in the car and drove to the next town where he got gas, and

Nellie watched him give the owner lots of samples for his customers. He paid for the gas before asking him where he could go to pay for a speeding ticket. The man told him he was the justice of the peace and to step inside. Dad and Nellie followed him into the gas station. He opened a door that Dad said had a desk and some chairs. The justice of the peace asked to see the ticket. Dad gave it to him and was asked if the officer might have made a mistake. Dad said he replied, "No! He looked like an honest man, and if he said I was over the speed limit, I must have been." He replied, "It is nice to see an honest person." I am not sure what else happened, but Dad left the "courtroom" with the ticket dismissed.

Nellie was dropped off at her brothers and promptly wrote a letter to Mom. When Dad got to his hotel room, he wrote a letter to Mom. Mom got a letter from Dad that as the old lady had never been in a fast car, he had driven faster than he should have and had been arrested and had no idea of where the old lady was. Mom had an idea that Dad wasn't telling the truth. Mom then got a letter from her mom, Nellie, what Dad had done as far as speeding, but the letter had Dad arrested and her left in a small town not knowing how to get to her brother's. As the letters were sent via the mail, Dad arrived home a day or two later. Dad told the whole story. Neither he nor Nellie had collaborated about the letters in advance. Each had come up with a story, using the facts, and as they were different but similar, Mom had thought they were true.

I am Anna's mother, Florence Ann Neese, a full-blooded Cherokee, and was born October 11, 1875. I married Nickolas McCullough on September 26, 1895, in Indiana, who had come from Ireland to fight in the American-Indian war. When the war was over, so many of the soldiers wanted to stay in the USA, and one way they could do that was to marry an American. We had our daughter December 20, 1897, in Indiana so she is half Cherokee. Than we moved to Oklahoma, which is where Anna would meet George. They met at the grocery store and George would come over a bunch. They were married, then they took the train to Walla Walla, Washington, where George lived. He had come here for a family reunion. The Preston family had come west with their own wagon train in the late 1800s. They settled in Preston, Washington. George moved to Walla Walla.

Very quickly Anna gave birth to her first child, Earl, then two years later gave birth to Clyde, my dad, and three years later while trying to give birth to their third, a son named Vernon, they both died about two weeks later. If I had been there, they would not have died. We Cherokee know how to help other women give birth. Five years later, George remarried a woman named Velma. She had started as the housekeeper. They would meet at Natatorium Dance and Hall. It had a swimming pool and was in Newport; Velma had worked for the phone company. They gave birth to four more children: Phillis, Kenneth, Sharron, and Francis.

I am taking over again. My father, George, was a horrible dad. So I learned what not to do. He beat us kids whenever he wanted, which was quite often. One time my two-year-old brother, Ken, was acting out. Ken was too loud for my dad, so my dad yelled to Earl, "Shut him up." Earl was starting it when this man went and got his strap and started to beat Ken in the face, back, and neck. I took the strap away. This horrible man went to the coal burning fireplace and grabbed the poker and started to hit Earl. Earl grabbed the poker from him, but in the shuffle Earl got a bloody nose. Earl went back and finished breakfast. This man was so angry, he said, "When you leave, don't ever come back." I was scared and when we went to school, I asked my brother, "Are you going to come home today?" He said, "Yes."

Well, one day "this man" showed us a $10 bill, something rare in those days. I saw him hide it and told my brother. Earl went in some time later and took it and bought lunch and two wristwatches. I asked my brother not to tell Dad that it was me who showed it where it was hidden. So my brother insisted that I had to fill the wood box and coal box for three months. Later our dad found out that Earl had taken the money and got his razor strap and beat the hell out of Earl. Another day Dad told us when we get home to cut back the berry bushes, Earl said, "Too much work. Let them grow another week." So Dad said, "Earl, *you* will do it today." When Velma moved, in she was able to calm down my dad and change his demeanor. We started to have a more normal life. Thank you, God! It helped us both, especially Earl, because he had taken the brunt. She was the one who taught me how to be a parent. I am so grateful for her; she helped me become a great parent. A few years after Phillis, Sharron, and Kenneth were born, we move to the ten-acre farm where we started to raise apples then wheat and vegetables.

One time Earl almost killed me. Uncle Limon had bought us both a gun. One day my brother hid behind an apple box and hit me in the butt several times. So I turned and hit him between the eyes with my hands. He then picked up a rock and slammed my right foot. It was a couple of weeks before I could walk again as I should.

Any money that we made had to be given to our dad so he could put it into the house. He told us, "I brought you into this world, and I can take you out."

At one point we both worked at SF Roosevelt Hotel and sold shoes, then I went to work for Schick. Earl asked why I would leave a job where I was very successful. A few years later, he asked me if Schick would bring him on. I was the top salesman at that point and was for most of the years I worked for them. We had always been competitive. One time we were about to go swimming and bet each other who would win. There was a bunch of people around and each bet on one of us. Earl said, "Whoever bets on Clyde will lose their money." Some people pulled out and he won that day. I thought I would beat him that day.

When I was about thirteen, there was a song called "My Dad," and my dad said it would be nice if you kids were to write a song about him. So I know our dad would be very pleased with my sister, Ann, for insisting and waiting over a year for some of us siblings to write these beautiful memories of our dad. Thank you, Ann, for being so persistent. I am sure she got that trait from our father.

That's what I remember the most is around the dining room table after a holiday dinner, our dad would tell a story or a joke and get so tickled with his tales, and he would start giggling before he got to the punch line. As I remember seeing him being so delighted with himself, it brings a smile to my face and many tears in my eyes.

As a salesman with a very large territory, there were other ways I made money. I made money at golf, pinochle, and as a rum runner. Actually, I would run anything. Every Monday when I started my trip, my car was filled with stock that I could sell to my customers if they were low on the items. Also, I would give a bunch away, then on Friday, my car was virtually empty. What to do with the space?

In Nevada, liquor was much cheaper. If a bottle of gin was $8 in Sacramento, it was $5 in there, so I would charge $6.50 for the bottle. This was a win-win for both of us. Remember, I had to care for a family of nine; Nellie Ruthie's mother lived with us and six kids. I kept it in two different areas; one for liquor and one for my betting. These were for my bride and me for special events. I really was an amazing golfer. I would only play one time a week, early Saturday morning, but was a scratch player. Why these guys would bet with me, I do not know. I had six holes in one. 1 I should not count, but I do. I was golfing in Monterey, I hit the ball and a seagull, picked it up and dropped it in the hole. I had only hit the ball once! The others were legitimate. Did I ever tell you how very remarkable I am?

My weekends were for me, but more importantly for my family. Yes, I played golf early Saturday morning, and pinochle late Saturday night. Friday night was pizza night, at least for a stretch. We would sit around the TV in the family room, no food in the living room till the kids were older, and watch the fights. We would bet but just for fun. My son Tom really liked this time with his dad, and my wife loved having me home. Remember when I walk through the door, she would hand me the keys of the boss of the house to me! Saturday after golf, we would all do something special. It would depend on what time of year it was. In summer, we would go to Folsom Lake and relax, swim, and take the boat out. We had been there so many times, we stopped looking around. I saved a life there too. Remember, I am a terrific swimmer, but what am I not terrific at? It was a time for our family to be together and for me to watch them grow. My bride always did a great job with the kids. I still do not know how she could run a large house, take care of six kids, and still be so energetic when I got home.

My name is Connie Spears and the best memory of Mr. P when I was growing up is when I went over there to see Ann. (Heaven help me if it was around dinnertime!) I would walk in and everyone would be gathered at the table, and Mr. P, with his soft, gentle voice, would say, "Are you hungry?"

My answer would be a timid "no."

Then he would say, "Have you had dinner yet?"

"No," I would say softly.

"Well, sit down and Ruthie fix her a plate." Oh, not just a little portion to tide me over till I got home to have my dinner, but rather a portion that would feed me and two others.

Another memory I have of Mr. P was when Jerry, Jeff, and I went there for a visit and after "dinner." (Seems like you're always having dinner at the Prestons'.) Mr. P fixed cherries jubilee. Jerry thought that was great, so when we got home he would have to do the same thing for anyone that would come to our house for the next month. I will always cherish my memories of Mr. P.

We are Veta, Ruthie's sister, and my husband Fred. What I liked about Clyde was vulnerability near enduring, his kindness that he tried so hard to hide, his devotion to his siblings, his childlike curiosity about new things to be discovered and explored, and his concern for people that were hurting. Your handsome father, I loved him.

Fred told me, "Clyde was my very best friend from the first day I met him. I liked him and his friendly, outgoing personality and his concern." His death was a real blow for me. I enjoyed every visit we had with him in California or in North Dakota. He was a gentleman and had many friends. I doubt that he had any enemies. He will be missed by everyone that knew him.

When your mom called and told me about Clyde, Fred said, "He was my very best friend and I can't stand it."

I am Aaron Baxter and there are so many things that remind me of Clyde. He was like a father to me. I could always count on him for the advice and guidance I needed. Ten years ago, when Valerie and I just moved to Sacramento and I was starting a new job, I met a rough, burly-looking man in a Safeway parking lot. I asked the man for directions to another Safeway store in the Reno area. The man not only gave me directions, but he had me follow him there in his car. When we arrived at the store, we both went inside and when it was time for me to talk to the manager about my order, this man took me by the hand, introduced me to the manager and told him, "Jay, take care of my little buddy." That man was Clyde. That was the start of a ten-year friendship. Clyde was one of the nicest tough guys you would ever want to meet. He would give you the shirt off his back. He was one of those rare individuals that really cared about his fellow mankind and the world we live in.

The thing I remember most about Clyde was his way to keep everything in perspective. Following my mom's death, she had been suffering from cancer for almost a year. I will never forget what Clyde said: "Little buddy, don't worry about your mom. She is at peace now and will no longer be suffering anymore pain. God rest her soul." Then he sat me down and started to ask a lot of questions than listen my answers: "Did you have a favorite place to go to dinner?" "What did Peggy do to make Christmas so special?" "What about Easter?" What was Peggy's family like?" "What would she do to make you laugh?" These and a dozen more, and he would sit and listen to all of my answers. I am sure a psychiatrist could not have helped me more.

Clyde taught me that we could all be more humane to each other and make other's lives better. I know that I became a much better person, and when I got married a few years later, I was a much better husband and man. Thank you, Clyde!

Clyde always lived in the present tense and never dwelled on the past or what could have been. Therefore, I know that he is at peace. It does not make it any easier not to have him around. We have lost a loving husband and father, but most of all we have lost a very good friend who I will always miss and never forget.

We are Scott and Louise Harding. We met Clyde and Ruth before they were married. We live in LA, so would see them quite often. They would spend the night here on their way to Mexico or coming back. We only had two kids; they had six and my two loved when they were here and had a great time with their kids. Clyde was the catalyst that kept us all together. His passing, for the group, was the end of an era. The fun, the party was over. As long as he was alive, some of Uncle Daddy was too. When our baby died, he and Ruth came down to be with us. I have never seen a more caring man. Men usually do not know what to do, but your father was great. He continued to touch us and sit quietly and ask us questions. He helped us so very much.

Cammie, our daughter, went to Rancho with her husband, Bobbie, to visit and she said they were not there ten minutes when Clyde had Bobbie out in the back building their fence. He was incorporated into the family. Thirty-seven years of constant contact. We had more of a life in Rancho than we had down here.

Clyde flew into LAX one Saturday for a meeting that week. I picked him up from the airport and brought him to Pacoima. From then on, he created havoc in our lives. He flipped a cigarette in the dark and it landed on a lounge pad, where it smoldered for two days. Sunday, we went to Han and Chris' for dinner and he helped himself to a bunch of peaches that he could reach on the tree, claiming he would take them home on the plane, but he did not. He left them with me. He had a meeting at the Hollywood Roosevelt, so we took them there and he told Scott where to park. He did and we got a $6 ticket, which was a fortune then. Clyde was persuasive, for sure. Monday, I put the peaches in a flat cardboard box to freeze. Tuesday, my eyes swelled shut at work and they sent me home in a cab. I missed a day of work, had to pay my doctor for a calcium shot, and was diagnosed of allergies to peace fuzz. Monday night, we had an exciting time putting out the fire that destroyed the lounge pad. It was a long time before we told Clyde how the fun of his visit lasted and lasted. He said something like "You must hate to see me come down." However, the truth is we loved to see him and spend time with him.

I am Joe Fitzsimons and I manage a King Soopers in Reno. When Clyde would come to my store, my staff was totally excited. We all knew that he would brighten our day. He had a different story every time he came in and they were all good. No matter what, we all ended up laughing. His racks were right between two checkout registers. So when working between them, he would tell his story. Then he would move to the next, so two clerks would laugh and the rest waited their turn. As laughter traveled through the store, the workers in the back and in the aisles would find a way to come to the front and hear him. What was so amazing is most of them were people in Clyde's life. We all loved that big galoot!

I am Fred Colombini and I have a great story. Clyde Preston, the godfather of our daughter, Victoria. That was one of the proudest days of his life and ours too. He normally would not go to church but did that day, and Monsignor Dwyer even asked the roof not fall in.

On a trip to Southern California while visiting San Juan Capistrano Mission, I heard a voice call my name: "Mr. Colombini." I reached for my wallet as I am sure I had dropped it. We were eight hundred miles from home and I knew that no one knew me there. It was Billy yelling my name out of one of the church windows. We went around the building and met Ruthie, Billy, and the others. They said Clyde was taking a nap in the trailer. Billy went out and got his dad, not telling him who he had found, and made Clyde pay admission to get into the church ground. Clyde was somewhat up set to have to pay to see me and my family. We only lived six blocks away in Rancho. We talked at the water fountain and decided to meet later that day at San Clemente State Park.

On a Fourth of July, on a camping trip to Lake Alamo, we had a great time on the new rubber boat. Ruthie had to return to work. We continued our trip to Oregon camping out in the trailer. One night at Grand Pass, the second was at Gold Beach, then we took a trip up the coast to look at Whaler Rock and this is where Fred did his famous snake dance getting away from a garter snake. The next night was at Clear Lake. We tried fishing again but not even a nibble. The girls are sure there are no fish.

The luck of Clyde! He and I worked for the same company but different divisions. We would plan some trips together and meet in Reno. The hotel were we stayed was the Royal Inn at Keystone and Seventh Street had a monthly drawing. Sure enough, Clyde won a two-and-a-half-ton car floor jack. Another time at the Eagle thrift store at 8:15 am, he walked in and there was $100 bill lying on the floor in front of him.

Clyde would buy liquor for his Elk buddies and would have the company car loaded to the brim. And the deal he made with them for every case he would buy, they were to give him a miniature bottle, and that is how the miniature collection started; he had one of every kind. In addition to the liquor, he also a deal with a meat company and buy meat, deer salami, cheese in full rounds, especially blue, which he would sell at a profit, of course.

Every Thursday night, we would spend the night at Sierra House Inn at Lake Tahoe. We would meet at the Sahara for dinner. We were to meet at 5:30. Clyde would always say, "Where the hell have you been?" He would have our coupons for $1 off the buffet and for free drinks. Thursday was German night. I sure got tired of bratwurst, but Clyde love those sausages. Instead of leaving a tip, he would give them razors or blades, even the bartender. That way, we never had to wait in line for dinner. The help knew what Clyde had in his pockets for them. After dinner, we would we play a few games of keno than go back to hotel and take a sauna.

When Clyde sprayed for spiders at his house, he would come to mine and spray. I guess he did it for a bunch of other neighbors. He would also check for termites under his house.

Clyde was always trying to get me to invest in penny stock. He was quite good at this, probably due to his luck!

Most of the time I went to Clyde's, he would make his famous Tom Collins. After three of these drinks, you would get grass stains on your knees crawling back to your car. We were also invited to their home many times for dinner. We fell very close to the Preston family. Cioppino dinner was one of his best. Clyde would work for three days to prepare it. Boy, was it great, and another was his beans, fabulous, and at times he would make bread with yeast and with a culture he started.

However, I saved the best story for last: the day I met Clyde. It was in a courtroom. His daughter, Ann, had been babysitting our three boys for a couple of years. We went to the New York World's Fair for several days. When we got home, we found that there had been a fire in our kitchen. We had just obtained an electric stove to replace our gas one, and Ann was used to a gas. One of the meals we wanted Ann to make included french fries. She had made them before. But this time when the oil started to smoke, she turned off the stove but did not know electric burners stay hot, and she continued with the rest of the meal. She turned around and found that the oil was on fire. She looked for the lid but could not find it then corn starch and flour. When we had bought the new bigger stove, we rearranged the kitchen. So Ann decided to carry the pot outside, so she opened the back door and started to carry out the pan. Well, as she did, some of the grease fell on the floor. She put it back on the stove, picked up the rug under her feet, and put out the fire. The pan of fire had started to burn our new cabinets. Still a burning pan, she took the boys out front and made them hold their hand as they were standing around a tree. She then ran to a neighbor's home—no one was there as it was a Fourth of July weekend—then to a second—no one. Going to a third, a car drove by and she stopped them. They went to the fire department and soon three trucks arrived. Ann took our boys to her house and for two and a half days stayed at her house. When we told our insurance company that we needed a rebuild, they decided to sue the Prestons' company. So at court they decided that Ann was not at fault and our company had to pay the bill. Well, when it was over, Clyde introduced himself to me and invited us to our first dinner at their home. He found out that I was a salesman and started to teach me, then got me to work for his company. Do you like this story?

I am Steve Barker. Ann, I received your letter on the second of August and want you to know I am flattered just to be included in your request. I thought about your late father and the many experiences we had over the years. Clyde was a very special kind of man that was cut from a rare breed. By that, I mean the more I got to know him, the more I began to realize what a complex character he was. He could cuss with the best of them, yet on the other hand he got misty-eyed just telling me of the honor he experienced being asked, with your mom (Ruth), to be godparents of Freddy and Kathy's daughter. He was forever saving a buck and bargain hunting, like the liquor runs for the Elks Lodge, and yet he was very generous with all that he had. He never once bragged about it, though. When working up in Reno, we often chatted in his room at day's end at the hotel on Keystone, and Clyde was forever messing with the seashells he had collected down in Mexico with Ruth. As often as we saw each other, the man would still insist on sharing car stock with me. He sure would be upset with me now that I started to grow a beard and the razors don't get the workout they're used to.

Now, let me tell you about the drive-in movies. Boy, was that fun—one flat rate for a car, not for each person in the car. When we started, there would be me, my bride, and four kids. We would go early in the summer so the kids could play in their playground, which was loaded with tons of fun things. We had a swing set with two swings, a slide, and a climbing area, and they had tons of things to play on, so all the kids could have fun at the same time. We would bring our popcorn and drinks. We parked close to the bathrooms because the kids, especially the girls, would need to use them. Tom very seldom would use their restroom. The big scream was wonderful and sound right in your car. Another thing we would do on the weekend evenings is to teach the kids how to dance. Ann was the best. One time at the Sacramento Inn, Stan Kenton and his group was performing. Ann and her date got up to dance. Slowly at first, those dancing around them stopped and started to make a circle around them to watch the two dance, until all the others, several hundred, stopped dance and made a huge circle. Ann and her date were the only two dancing. When the song was over, everyone clapped and cheered "Great job!" "Wonderful!" "Magnificent!" and it was not for Stan Kenton. This was not the only time people would stop and watch Ann dance, but it was the only time that everyone in the room stopped.

I remember the birth of each of my children, but the birth of my first one, Tom, was the most exciting. I did not know how the hospital operated. My only experience I had was the birth of my brother with a midwife. My stepmother remembers when my mother died when giving birth to my younger brother, she was screaming so loud it scared me to death. Now in the hospital, they keep you in the waiting room so you don't hear any screaming.

My daughter Ann had a very unique experience giving birth to her only child, Paul. Scott's father was dying, so he asked Ann to get an ultrasound to find out the sex of the child so he could tell his dad. She did even though she did not want to know the sex of her child until the child was born, but she did. When they did the ultrasound, they discovered that Ann had a condition: placenta previa. Had Paul been born through the birth canal, it could have ripped off his head, arms, or legs. Anyway, Paul was scheduled to be born on May 28. On the morning of March 17 at 4:00 am, Ann woke up and discovered that she was hemorrhaging. She screamed for Scott, and he called the hospital, got Ann into the car, and sped to the hospital. Ann was scared that he would be pulled over by the police—that did not happen. When they arrived, there was a gurney waiting for Ann to get her to the operating room. They ran the gurney down the halls, quickly got her prepared with tubes and things on both arms which were both pulled out, and left the room to get everything ready. Ann said as she lay there, she remembered Christ on the cross and she prayed, "Father, if you choose that I should not live, please take care of my son, Paul." When she woke up, she was told of the story of Paul's birth.

Her doctor, while doing a cesarean, was cutting very little and cauterizing. Ann tends is a bleeder. The doctor went in to get Paul, but he slipped under Ann's ribs and his head hit Ann's heart, which stopped beating. The doctor slit her open, grabbed Paul, and screamed for a team waiting outside the room in case Paul needed the extra help. If they did not come into the room, they would not have been paid the team. So Ann found out that when her son was born, he killed her. Not many kids kill their parents especially at such a young age. Paul only weighed when born was three pounds five ounces, very small. She was in the hospital for a week and they kept Paul for five and a half weeks. On April 20, they told her that she could take her son home tomorrow, and she screamed, "*No*, he only weighs four pounds five ounces. He has to weigh five pounds for me to take him home." They said, "We have watched you and you will do fine." Well, he ate around the clock every three hours. He would drink less than one ounce of milk to start with from a very small bottle with a big hole in the nipple. So births have really changed!

My wife's grandmother was a midwife in Bisbee, North Dakota, and delivered over 125 babies and never lost a mother or a child. In the 1800s, usually one out of five would die, she never lost one child or mother. She was written up in the local paper not only as a midwife but all the other things she did for so many people in the town: "Grandma Irmen will really be missed."

The following night, Dad plugged in the lights and got ready for a Christmas party for the adults. The doorbell rang and Dad opened the door to see a bearded man in a black suit. He didn't ask who he was. He turned and yelled, "Son of a bitch, Ruthie, the rabbi is here for you." Mom didn't believe Dad but came to the door. I don't remember his name, but the rabbi and Father Dwyer attended the Christmas parties for several years. Everyone wanted to attend Dad's parties.

XXXXXXXXXXXXX

My name is Racheal Williams and my husband Bill met Clyde when he first moved to Sacramento. Ruthie's mother lived with them for the first time and she was a bitch from hell, and it did not bother Clyde at all. Ruthie was not happy about it, but it did not bother Clyde at all; he was the only one that tolerated her. He really said she did not bother him. But there was almost nothing that bothered him. He was truly amazing. Bill and I could never understand how anyone could be so great. Everyone that met Clyde thought the same thing. He made our lives better!

I am Lesley Sprat and I grew up with Mary, the Prestons' third kid. I, like everyone else, love going to there. Their home life was really amazing. I was amazed that they never fought; they all got along so well. I never saw any other mom and dad love each other so perfectly. The way try support to each other, looked at each other, and touched each other. So many people could learn so very much from them. I learned to be a better wife and a mother than my mom because of what I learned over the years. I asked my mom why she did not do so many things Mary's mom did. She thought I was making it up; no one could possibly do all those things and never fight.

We welcomed many friends and neighbors to our home for dinner. So many times it was our kid's friends and our neighbors. It is ever so much fun to have twelve to twenty-four people all sitting at the same table. Each added so much to our lives, so we became even more than what God had made of us. My kids thought that we did not go to other people's house because there were too many of us. The truth is that very few were as welcoming or had the money we had to entertaining as we were. Most did not have the big house we had with five bedrooms and a dining room that could set twelve or a rumpus room that could set twenty-four. Most did not have the dishes, silverware, and glasses that were needed for that many people.

During any vacation time, Christmas, Easter, or summer, we would enjoy entertaining a marinade of families. After my death, many went to my home and told many stories of the times they spent at our home with their families, and all the times we went to visit them. So that is why I am letting them tell all of these stories.

My name is Pidge, the one who scared Ann when they lived next to us in Red Wood City. I remember when Clyde would come to Reno, he would always come and pick me up so I could spend the day with him. He would take me into all the stores and it was most amazing that when he entered, every one of the employees got excited and started passing the word, "Clyde's here," "Clyde's here," "Clyde's here." He would take it all in stride and call each by name. If there was a new employee, Clyde would go up to him/her and say, "You must be new here, I have not seen you before, what is your name?" They would tell him so he would stick out his hand and say, "_____, good to meet you, please call me Clyde!" I have no idea how he could remember all of their names but he did, and I could not even though I was younger than him but it was because of my drug use. Clyde tried to get me away from the guys I hung out with. One time, he convinced me to go to his dad's in Walla Walla so that I could get away from the drugs. So I went but after a short while I hitchhiked back to Reno. It was the worst mistake of my life. I was too big for my britches. I started the biggest drug business that Nevada ever had and spent my life in prison. My trial lasted almost two complete years. I wish I had listened to him. All of his kids turned out great. They all learned to work hard and become so much like their dad.

I remember going to their home for a week in the summer. It was great; they had a real home. My mom married so many times I did not have a dad. When she was not married, there were so many guys that were there. Mr. and Mrs. Preston were so in love with each other and shared their love with everyone. It was our favorite time of the year. We never wanted to leave. Their meals were great and we all ate at the same time and at the same table. Now, my mom was a great cook but she did not have the money. Looking back, I was too stupid to learn how I should have lived.

Ann, Clyde's daughter, would come to visit me in prison when I was at Florence Maximum Security. She was so much like her dad, amazingly like her dad; never met a stranger. She had no problem coming to this place that had the worst criminals, like Dommer. At first she was able to bring her fabulous bread and cinnamon rolls, none better. It is the greatest bread in the world, truly. Ann would also visit my mother. As a matter of fact, she was the one that told my sister that Mom should not live alone as she had gotten so bad. My mom was afraid to turn on the stove or washing machine, so Jackie got Mom to move in with her. Ann saved my mom's life.

My son, Tom, was the only child of mine that went into the service. He went into the air force and not the navy like me, and he served in Vietnam. He was also awarded many times, and one time his plane was hit and shot down. They were able to land in an American-friendly country. He told me that night they all went out to a bar and had many drinks—too much adrenaline. This was amazing to me because Tom never drank! See how a war can change someone. They also did not know about PTSD than like they do now.

My grandson, Paul, also went into service. He chose the army. His mom, Ann, asked him not to go into the army or marines. Paul went to the air force and they wanted his diploma. He told them that he had a GED, and they said they wouldn't accept him. So he went across the hall, took the Army ASVAB test, and received an extremely high score. The recruiter took the test scores across the hall to the air force office and showed them what they had passed up. At that point, the air force recruiter said they would take Paul; he said no. The army wanted to put him in intelligence, but that required six years and Paul did not want that long, so he became a medic, the second-highest rank group. It turned out they stop-loss him so he served for almost eight years. Paul, like his mother, uncle, and me, saved lives.

It turned out that when his first sergeant Jesus Rodrigues came back for R&R, he put Paul in charge of all the doctors and medics. At that point Paul was a specialist, one grade above a private. He was in charge of sergeants, captains, and doctors. Ann asked those of higher ranks if they were upset that Paul was in charge, and all of them said, "*No*, Paul was the right one for the job." Anyway, only Paul and Tom went into the service.

My name is Jim Burris and I met Clyde when Ann and my best friend, Scott, got married. I was his best man, and there were many occasions that the family got together. What a great family. I never met a better one, and Clyde was as funny as hell. Clyde introduced me to Father Dwyer as the groom. It would not have been funny but in those days, white females did not marry black guys. Scott was late for our rehearsal.

Clyde always took care of everyone all the time. At the reception, Clyde had every type of alcohol and tons of wine and beer. There were four hundred guests and the reception lasted over four hours, and he did not run out of anything. Ruthie asked some of her friends to help with the food. She gave them the different receipts and the money to make them. She did not have enough room in their two refrigerators for all the dishes. Each brought the food to the recreation room before the wedding. That place had tons of refrigerators and room for more than four hundred to sit at tables.

After the wedding, all went to the recreation room and started partying while we stayed at the church and took more pictures, which took about a half an hour. When we arrived, a reception line was formed. Do you know how long it took for Ann and Scott to greet all of their guests? Well, Clyde brought them drinks. He always looked around to see what anyone needed. He always amazed me that he always looked around to see that everyone was taken care of. I wish my family was as great as theirs. Not only me but so many others thought the same thing.

When I went to dinner, Clyde would say, "I need my buddy to sit by me tonight." I found out that he treated everyone as if they were his best friend.

I am Captain Michael Morgan and I bought a house right next to the Prestons' in August of 1955 with my wife, Michael. We had two younger kids. We were there less than three years. I thought Mather Air Force Base would have kept me there longer or I would not have bought a house. The Prestons were great; all of them very generous and always sharing. They had an apple tree, banana trees, and almond that they gave to us neighbors.

Clyde was very generous when we had to sell our house; he gave us what we asked for it. Maybe because we had both been in the military and understood how money was so needed. I found out that when we moved, he moved the fence between our houses over ten feet so he could park his new RV in the backyard. Then he rented it out to other military for less than other houses were renting for. Clyde really was wonderful.

My name is Fred Smith and I worked with Clyde. He was the best teacher I had. Everything came naturally to him. He was a very hard worker, but he had been a hard worker all of his life. I do know that he knew how to relax. He loved pinochle and was always one of the winners, usually the big winner. When someone in sales started to work for Schick, they were usually set to Clyde for training for usually two weeks. He was the best teacher. I was from Florida and I flew to Sacramento to be with Clyde and did not come home on the weekend between the two weeks. It did not matter what store we went into; everyone was always excited to see him and that he was at their store. I have never seen anything like that before or since. Clyde treated everyone great and it did not matter if they were a clerk or the boss.

Most people who knew me believed me to be lucky, especially the ones I played cards with. Their disbelief at my luck left them with a variety of emotions. Sherm would get angry, Dr. Alan Kincaid would laugh, Paul would cuss, and Nellie would draw up her mouth in a tight pucker except if I were her partner, then she would beam from ear to ear. To set the record straight, I was not lucky; I was highly skilled! I knew the games and played them well. My two favorites were pinochle and bridge, though occasionally I would play poker and of course win. Skill was one of my greatest attributes. Understand however that skill is something I developed. Lazy people are never skillful because developing a skill takes a hell of a lot of hard work and they do not want to work. Skill is one of those things that one can be transferred from one area of your life to another. My father, God rest his soul, taught me (instilled in me) the benefit of hard work. My mother died when I was three and in the next ten years, my brother Earl and I were to learn a lesson: work. If she had been alive, I do not believe I would have learned so very much so very early. Even after my father remarried, I continued the hard work. Today, parents are too easy on their kids. When kids learn to work, they have a much better and easier life. I have tried to tell others that by making kids work, they learn. When the kids were picking up rocks, it was a game of who could get the most. With the grandkids picking up the nuts, it was a game, not work. Help your kids.

My name is Racheal Williams. My husband, Bill, met the Prestons when they first moved to Sacramento. Ruthie's mother lived with them for the first time and she was a bitch from hell and it did not bother Clyde at all. Ruthie was not happy with her mom, but Clyde was the only one that tolerated her. He really said she did not bother him. But there was almost nothing that bothered him. He was awesome. Bill and I could never understand how anyone could be so great. Everyone who met Clyde thought the same thing. He made our lives better.

I am Leslie Spratt. I grew up with Mary, the Prestons' third child. I, like everyone else, loved going over there. Their home life was truly wonderful. I never saw a fight when I was there, and I was there quite often. They all got along so very well. There was no other family I knew like them. This might be one reason that so many people loved going over there. I never saw any other mom and dad love each other so very much, the way they would look at each other, talk with each other, and hold each other. So many people could learn a great deal from that. I learned to be a better wife than my mother because of the example I saw. For many years, my mother did not believe me. She was sure that I was making it all up. She said, "No one could do all of those things and never fight." But when I got married, she said, "Leslie, you must have been telling me the truth about the Prestons because your life is much better than mine has been."

I am Dick Weaver and thank you for your letter and thinking of me of people to contribute something about your father, Clyde Elmer. I first met your parents when they were living in an apartment in Brisbane, California. Your dad was working at United Airlines. Both of your parents, in my book, were the most likable couple that I have ever met. One complemented the other, and I know Clyde had Ruthie in mind at all times. It was wonderful to witness. There are so many things that I can think of that makes me laugh but I don't think they could go into a book! Nothing was wrong. It was just the way we did it, like going to the NCO Club at Moffat Field, enjoying drinks at $0.25, and leaving with a case of beer concealed by my top coat with your mother holding on to my arm. She almost died when she found out what we had acquired. Another I recall is when Clyde Elmer, Jack, Frank, and I were going to Santa Cruz. We took off about 11–12 pm after your dad got through working at UAL with a couple cases of beer and a deck of pinochle cards. We stopped by at a café along the way. And by the time we left, the back seat was loaded with garden furniture and me. We had not gone too far to make a pee stop by the side of the road when a police car pulled up. They wanted to know if everything was all right. Clyde said everything was fine. It was just that Frank was a little sick. The police said "Okay," just take it easy. By that time, I had lost five pounds as I was in the back with the furniture. I could not run if I had to. Well, we got to Santa Cruz and could not find a place to sleep. Clyde finally said, "Now, that is a nice park." Over the wall we climbed, rolled up in our blankets, and went to sleep. I woke up at 6:00 am to the sound of sprinklers. Hell, we were sleeping on someone's front lawn and the man of the house was standing on the porch. The four of us did not climb over the fence; we cleared it with one jump. Yelling "sorry" to the man, we headed for the beach in Santa Cruz. There, we spread out the blanket, beer cooler handy, and started to play pinochle. Some people started to watch Clyde. Even some of them took out some beer and opened them for us. I am sure they knew they were serving Don Ameche. It was sunset when we picked up the cards, etc., and returned worse for wear.

I don't remember when your dad left UAL and went to work for Schick, but he was the best salesman they ever had. He knew his products, clients and how to sell them. I ask you who else could walk into a store and say "Hi, buddy boy" and have them love him. If I said something like that, I'd get knocked on my keester and thrown out. The reason that all new salesmen were set to Clyde for training is that he won many awards. He was exceptional. He worked ten to twelve hours a day except Friday. He would like to get home to his wife by 3 to 3:30. If he was out of town for two to three weeks, he would work Saturday and sometimes Sunday. Things I loved about him: He loved his wife and family. Without a doubt he was the most compassionate man I have ever known, not only on the outside but also on the inside. He was concerned about others at all times. Your father was great to all those he met. There has never been another like Clyde. I bet you are proud to call him Dad! I was proud to call him my friend and the best friend I ever had!

This is Pidge again and there are so many things I remember about Clyde that I could write a book myself. I was out visiting one day, bored to death and thought, "What the hell, I'll go and see if Clyde wants to shoot baskets. I'll beat that ole man easy. He likes to gamble so I will pocket some money too." Well, it started raining so we were confined to the house. "Now what?" I said. So Clyde threw a hat across the room and said, "Whoever can throw the most cards in the hat wins." I knew that this was going to be easy and I decided a penny a card would be fair. This went on for an hour or so and my pocket was getting empty and I was convinced that I could not win this game. Now, the weather stopped, so we went outside to shoot those baskets, at $0.25 per game, called horse. I had about $1.50 left on me, and we played about one hour and I think I won one game. The ole' man I thought was a pushover, had all my money and me thinking that I was an idiot for thinking I could beat him! Now I, being stubborn, still wanted to play, so four more games later and one more dollar down, I had to tell him that I didn't have the money to pay up. So I ended up under the house checking some air vents, for what reason I did not know, and scared to death because there were spiders, mud (yuck) under there. Never again did I bet against him on anything. After I came out from under the house, he was laughing his ass off and gave me back all my money . . . Clyde had more heart than an army, was as honest as a priest, and funnier than a clown. I loved that man, always have and always will. *God bless him.*

As I told you before, I saved four people's lives but finally six. The American Red Cross awarded me and others of our achievements at a banquet. Most of my family was there and quite a night. Congressman Robert T. Matsui wrote me a letter congratulating me. But that was not as big of a deal as George Bush wrote my daughter Ann two letters about what she had accomplished through Adopt a US Soldier, an organization she started when her son, Paul, first went to Iraq in 2004. He even sent a signed picture. I had the most wonderful family ever, and everyone we knew thought so too. You have heard from many of them but there are more to come.

My name is Pat Kirby, and my kids and I moved to Rancho in 1957. We lived a few blocks from the Prestons. I got to know them through my children going to the same school as their kids went. I had been divorced before we moved there and I also had to work outside the house. I worked at the local grocery store. There was only one when we got there and I was able to walk there. Clyde and Ruth were always willing to help take care of my kids for me on weekends if I had to work. My kids loved going over there because they ate so well. The Prestons always ate so very well and we did not; I did not have the money. Every Christmas, Clyde would ask me if I needed anything. I have never met anyone so generous. The kids followed suit and brought us apples, bananas, nuts, both walnuts and almonds, and a special treat, pomegranates, which they grew in their large yard.

We are Don and Edna Seitz. We lived next to Ann and Scott when they bought their first home in Rancho. It was a new neighborhood so all of us had lots of time to party, help each other with yard work, take care of kids, and whatever neighbors do for each other. When we moved in, Ann helped Edna almost every day, putting things away, taking care of the kids, and cooking for us. She said that she had learned this from her parents. They always treated neighbors like family. We had never experienced that before, but Ann made our neighborhood great, as we were told her parents had done the same in their neighborhood. All of us would have done so very much better if we had parents like Ann's. Our world would have been much better if that were the case! We would have had close to a perfect world. Would that have been wonderful? Now, Scott's family was horrible. His mother left when he was three and came back three years later. Scott, his brother, and sister never could go to sleep unless there was a light or TV on. *Sad!* Too many people grew up with horrible parents. That is the reason our world is in the shape it is. Please learn from this book to be better people. After we had been there a few years, we learned from Ann. If someone new moved in, Ann was always there to help them unpack all the boxes. If they wanted the dishes washed, she showed them how to wash and rinse in the sink and put them in the dishwasher to dry, leaving the door opened to dry faster, and then go do something else while they dried. Ann liked to make up the master's room early. When a new neighbor, Vicky, moved in, she told us that Ann insisted on making up her bed and she did not argue but thought it could wait. They continued to work, and Ann left about 5:00. She continued to work, and by the end of her day she said she was exhausted and was grateful that her bed was made so she was able to fall into it.

Hello, we are Dave and Darleen Hoffman, neighbors of Mary, third child of the Prestons, and her husband, Clark. We got to know them through their daughter, Kim, who went to school with our daughter, Angela. We lived down the street a bit. Mary's story was more than true. Clyde ran around the neighborhood and showed everyone how to get rid of weeds. He told us to give our kids a table knife and showed them how to use it. They were all pretty excited to do something wonderful. We were all amazed. Then he asked them what else they could use to get rid of the weeds. Then it started: screwdriver, spoon, fork, dead tree branch, sharp rock. The kids liked going out and sharing with the other kids something new to get the weeds out. We did get the weeds out and our kids asked if there was something else they could do. Amazed as hell, we found out how Clyde and Ruth had such great kids. They also had such strong family ties. Clyde also made lots of work fun, so the kids actually liked to work. This one thing helped to change our lives. Great job!

We are the Sorensens, Jeff and Wanda. We have known Clyde and Ruth for over forty years. We would visit them yearly or they would come to our home. We were not fortunate to have kids but we were so impressed how they raised their kids. Their kids never lied, and we were amazed. We knew that many families and their kids would lie from time to time, but not the Prestons'. We have no idea what they did to achieve this. How did they train them? I wish the world knew how to raise kids. Wanda and I talked about it after visiting other families. We watch their kids lie or misbehave. We thought it could be the immense love each had for the other. That immense love was missing from so many families. Also, Clyde and Ruth would put two or three kids on the same job so they learned how to depend on each other and get great results. We thought that could also make a difference. It could also be because they did so very many things together as a family, not only at night but all the wonderful trips they would take. They did so many things together as a family. Their family was #1 and always welcomed everyone. I heard of one time Clyde had a bunch of people over—friends, neighbors, a living room full of people. There was a knock on the door and Clyde opened the door, Clyde had never seen this guy before and asked, "What is your name?" The guy said his name was Ben, and he wanted to see Ann. Well, Clyde invited him in and introduced him to everyone. Ben was offered a chair and he sat down. Clyde offered him a drink but Ben said, "No, thank you," and he sat quietly. Well, after a while, Ben said he would have to go. When Ann got home, her dad said, "Ben stopped by to see you." Ann had no idea who this Ben could be. Ben never came back. I am sure he was blown away.

My mother, Elizabeth, already told you about what Uncle Clyde and Aunt Ruth did for our family, which was absolutely amazing. I am Nelly and I was six years old when we came to live with them. Now that I am older, married, have kids of my own, I can hardly believe it. First thing that struck me is that they always had food and a lot of it! Also, for the first time I found out what leftovers were. We never had leftovers. In North Dakota, we did not have a lot and I know the Preston kids did not know how lucky they were. My mom and dad loved each other as much as Uncle Clyde and Aunt Ruth.

This was the first time I had to do chores. Katheryn, my older sister, usually did all the work back home. Here, we all had to work. At first I did not like it at all. Then I learned how it connected us and brought us closer together, and that was great and I felt better about myself. I could do things. I like that. There was one thing: Uncle Clyde scared me. I used to wet the bed and Uncle Clyde said he would beat my ass if I did it again. My mom, sister, and Ann would get me up and get me to the bathroom when I had been in bed a few hours. I was saved.

Slowly, my mom got better, never 100 percent but maybe 95 percent. That was wonderful for all of us. My mom continued to go to the doctor and Aunt Ruth usually drove her. We were so greatly taken care of and we all loved that. They finally discovered that my mother had a brain tumor just like her dad had. I remember her falling to the ground and foaming at the mouth; I was scared to death. The seizures finally stopped and we were all so happy.

Ann was at the hospital when my mom died. She told me how beautiful my mom's death was. My mother could hardly speak but said to Ann, "God really loves you." Ann said she said to my mom, "Aunt Elizabeth, God really loves you and that is why he is coming to take you to heaven." At that moment, she died. It was so nice to know that her death was beautiful and peaceful.

I am George Brown. Clyde served under me when he was in the navy; I was his major. We appreciate everyone's service but we really appreciated Clyde's service. He was our go-to guy. Whatever anyone wanted or needed, they would go to him and Clyde would get it. He did not care about the rank of the person asking; he would get for everyone. It made him happy to make others happy. I never met anyone before or after Clyde that cared so very much. Clyde would look a person in the eyes and say "_____. I know that after yesterday you could really use a little something. What can I get for you?" Only commanders would say that for those under him. The way Clyde took care of everyone was like he was the commander. Some of my fellow officers said the same thing when we got together. We all thought that your dad was great. I am glad that you are writing a book about him. The world should know there are some truly great and fabulous people in the world.

I'm Sgt. Williams. I, too, served with Clyde during World War II. I do not know how he did it but he was great to everyone, especially me. When I was there, I found out that my wife had been killed in a car accident. We had been out on a long mission. It was tragic for me. I heard that the funeral was over and she had been buried. The first thing Clyde did was buy me a bottle of bourbon and he would sit with me nightly for a week. He would ask poignant question and sit and listen to me. The first question he asked me was, "Please tell me, sergeant, what was the favorite thing you and June liked to do?" It made me cry remembering my wife in my arms. How will I live without her? Then tons of more questions: "What made Christmas special?" "What about Easter?" "What would June do for your birthday?" "Did you take and special trips?" "What was her family like?" "How did you meet?" There were so very many questions. By the end of the week, I was feeling so very much better. I found out that I would be able to live. Clyde saved my life; there was no one like him.

Well, I am Mary Slattery and I was with your mom when she met your dad. I do know that your parents are my favorite couple. Your dad was fun-loving, silly at times, generous, sweet, soft-spoken, and always a gentleman. I know that your mother was very much in love with him. I wish we had lived closer through the years so we could spend more time together. Iowa is a long way from California and with us having six kids, we just could not afford the trip. No extra money; it wasn't possible! Your father had a great sense of humor and a wonderful laugh. Dick and I hope to get to California when we retire. I met Dick when I was living with your mother. It's amazing that she and I met our spouses when we were living together. They were both in the navy, and Clyde introduced me to Dick. Dick was on a ship that came into San Francisco several times. I was also glad I lived with your mother because I was so far from home, very naive, and only nineteen years old, and your mom was much older, twenty-three, I believe. I do not know what I would have done without your mother. We had some double dates and they were fun. Your dad was always having fun. A lot of water has passed under the bridge since 1945–1946. She was the bridesmaid at my wedding and I was hers. She got married before me, and I not too long after her. I had our first child before Ruth had hers.

We are Jake and Virginia Dugan. There are lots of things I remember: going to the Elks Club for a steam bath, sauna, golf game, playing bridge, driving everyone else up on the wall because we did not have an orthodox manner. Generally, Ann, your dad was just a great guy, and Virginia and I loved him. Your dad's language was not the most flowering, yet he got away with it. Once in a while, I saw Ruthie looking at him saying, "Clyde." He got a sheepish grin on his face and talked himself out of it. When each of you children were born, he'd be proud as punch as he would say something like "Well, that's quite a piece of work" or "She really is something, isn't she?" But his hands were gentle as he held a child and his loving eyes were showing his pleasure and love.

He used to play bridge with either Ruthie or Nellie. He was so very lucky. He could play his cards, but boy, was he lucky. One time, your grandmother asked him how come he would get the cards he needed, and he said, "I just ask the Lord to help me." We all laughed because we knew how Nellie would get provoked! He was one of a kind. In a little town of Eldred, Pennsylvania, with a population of two thousand five hundred, I talked to my uncle's next-door neighbor. I told him we lived in California. He said he did too. I asked where, and he said Rancho Cordova. I said we had old and dear friends living there on Barbara Street. He said, "I live on the same street." I told him they're Clyde and Ruth Preston. He said, "Clyde only live a couple houses away from us. He was some guy." The fellow's name was Abladinger and he hadn't been there for several years but he did remember your dad and that he was great.

I never liked to hear anyone swear all the time or say things, etc., but the funny thing with Clyde, I don't know, and don't get me wrong, but Clyde would only make me laugh while he'd say some of his choice expressions. He loved to get a reaction, good or bad. He was all things you want to write about and he was humorous, generous, tender, and a loving person.

We are Thelma and Clay and we enjoyed all the times the Elks group got together. We did so many things; bridge was one of my favorite, but Clay liked the fishing trips. We had so much fun together. Clyde and Ruth had the biggest house; we would go there so many times. I will always remember the phone calls. If I answered the phone, I would say, "Just a moment, I will get Clay." Your dad would say, "Hell, I really don't want to talk to the old bastard; I'd rather talk with you." Yes, that was Clyde all right: a beautiful, wonderful guy. Clay would say they threw away the mold when they made Clyde. I have enclosed a couple of pictures; one is of the Mendenhall's fiftieth anniversary party at your home and we had your dad's fantastic cioppino dinner.

When we first moved to Rancho Cordova in 1955, Fourth of July weekend, my bride would have to drive about eight miles to the closest church. In those days, they had to fast from midnight if they were to receive communion, so they would go to the earliest mass. While they were there, I would make breakfast. I was also a great cook. Remember, my mom died when I was three and I became the main cook. I did not go to church with them; I had been baptized First Baptist in the Pacific Ocean. I made sure it was big and wonderful. The kids loved Sunday breakfast because there was almost every hot food available, and just like dinner, they got to choose. There were always eggs and most of the time bacon or sausage, and either pancakes or waffles, not both, and toast, at least one type of fruit, and three types of juice or milk. Many times I would make biscuits; those were a treat like a dessert. I did not ever make or serve donuts; we seldom had them. In the olden days, potatoes were seldom served. But the most important was when my wife got home, I had a cup of coffee waiting for her as she entered the door. Did I tell you I truly was a loving, devoted, and hardworking husband? Anything to let my bride know "*I am here for you*!" I would also make bacon, sausage, and eggs many different ways. Many times I would cut up fruit so when the food was passed, everyone would take the amount of whatever they wanted. There was a twelve-year range of age between the kids. Of course the older ones would eat more. The older ones were also more appreciative of the goodies we served.

This summer was when we first met our new neighbors. We live across the first park in Rancho and it was a full block. When we first moved there, it was a grape vineyard. Soon, they cleared it and made a great park for the kids to play and us to have picnic meal!

This is when we met our new neighbors as they move in; we were the first on the block. Our first was Captain Michael Morgan and his family lived to the right of us if you were looking at the park across the street and we were looking west! He had two young boys that Ann helped take care of. He was not happy when he was moved to another base; he thought they would be at Mather for years.

The reason why Rancho was built was that Mather Air Force Base was getting so big, so they built the big town. As the end of the first two years, there were about fifty thousand people. Now, we are talking over two million.

We also welcomed many friends and relatives to our home; it seems there was always somebody there. Many times it was my kids' friend and our neighbors. It is ever so much fun to have dinner with twelve to twenty people. Each added so much to our lives. So we made room and became more than God had made us. My kids thought we did not go to others often because there were too many of us. The truth is that very few are as welcoming and had the money we had to entertain in a great way. Also, most did not have a five-bedroom home with very large room that we had. Our formal dining room would seat twelve, and the rumpus room would set up to twenty-four with no problem all at one table. We also have the dishes, glassware, and silver to accommodate them all.

During vacation times, Christmas, Easter, and summer, we would have a myriad of families. After my death, many came to the house and told many stories of the times they would visit us or we would visit them. All were very good stories. You have already read some and here are some more.

We are Michael and Nancy Meyers. We met the Prestons when the first Catholic church in Rancho opened up. We met Ruth and her kids first. It was a small church that was changed into a hall when the big church was built. How could you miss a mom with a bunch of kids? Our kids and theirs played together all the time because they also attended the school at St. John Vianney. That was a great school. At first there was only second through sixth grade. And each year they would add one year to the top and bottom till they had kindergarten through eighth grade.

We wanted to meet both parents so we would know our kids were safe when they're over there. We stopped over one weekend and found that not only would our kids be safe but they had a much happier home than we did. We learned so much from Clyde and Ruth. One thing we learned was to do lots of things together as a family; it made the family closer to each other. They were always doing things as a family. Until we went over, we would just have some meals together. We changed that and started to do things together on weekends. It took a while to share many more things. They made our lives better and we are so very grateful for them.

I am Aaron Buboes and I met Clyde when I was up in the mountain at Ann's house. We were all drinking and Ann had the biggest bar with more different kinds of liquor than the three liquor stores in Fairplay, Colorado. It was wonderful because after being in at war in Iraq for over a year, we needed to relax. I think there were twelve of us there that weekend. Clyde had a drink with us and started to talk. He had been in World War II, so he knew what we were going through. He started to talk, asked us a bunch of questions, and made us share the worst things that happened to us. That was amazing because it helped us feel better. I cannot remember all questions but the longer he talked, the better I was feeling and the slower I was drinking. I thought that he should go to AA, but I and the others would not have gone to AA. He made a great change in our lives. After we left there, we would start to talk about all we experienced during the week and I know we all drank less. What a great lesson. Thank *you*, Clyde. You are great. You helped me a great deal!

Hello, I am Bob McFarland and I was a competitor of Clyde's. I worked for Gillette. Schick was not a better company than Gillette but Clyde was a better salesman than me. He was kind and tried to show me how to make people really listen to me. He was great. He told me that anyone that bought Gillette would stick with them and the same with Schick, but the clerks were the ones that made the difference. You make friends with the clerks and store workers and they will say to the customer, "I know you always buy Gillette, but have you ever tried Schick? I like them better." I am afraid he told me too late because all the stores we both went into were totally sold on Clyde. They loved him so very much. However, there were stores I had that he did not go into and I saw the difference it makes. Clyde was so happy to help everyone around. I never met a person like him. I loved to watch him and learned so very much from him and all his actions. After the time with him, I tried to teach other sales reps to do the same. Hopefully, I was able to help others. There was no one as great as Clyde.

We are Jen and Jim Glesing. We met in high school but did not get married till after college. We were friends of Tom and would go over there to do homework. If we were there for a long time, we would be invited to stay for dinner. That never happened at any other home. Both Jim and I preferred going there to do homework for that reason and that Tom was one of the smartest guys in our class. The whole family was so very friendly; we never met another like them even to this day. It made us a better couple and family when we got married. We learned how a family should really be. Why in the world were there not more families than the Prestons in this world? We not only learned from smart Tom but the entire family. You expect to learn when you are in school, but Jim and I learned how to be better people after we got married. Our family was much better than Jim's and mine. So very glad we got to know Tom and his family!

I am Chris Grant. My wife, Kathy, and I first met Clyde years ago. We were walking out of a liquor store with a nice bottle of champagne. It was our anniversary, and he said, "Nice bottle, would you like me to join you?" We were both amazed and said, "Sure." Well, he followed us to our house and we had a great time. Also, this took place in the '50s and at that time you could trust a stranger, which could not happen nowadays. He entertained us, telling stories about his wife and three kids. We could tell he loved his family. He asked us many questions, about how we met, how long we have been married, where we born and raised in Boise, and many others. Then he sat and listened to us. It made this anniversary one of our best. Clyde was really a wonderful guy; he cared about others and he made our days better. We never met anyone like him. From time to time when he was in Boise, he would come over for dinner and we would introduce him to some of our neighbors, and they all thought he was great.

Our youngest brother, Bill, recently died, and this is what they wrote about him: "Bill Preston, fifty-three, of Klamath, passed peacefully in his sleep. Our brother would greet each day with a heartfelt good morning shout to his friends and neighbors. He was intelligent, kindhearted, and fun-loving, a jokester, a great storyteller, and a master of inventions. He loved gold panning, fishing, camping, and diving for abalone. He enjoyed gambling; Elk Valley knew him as "*big money*." He will be missed by all. During the Blackberry Festival, he totally enjoyed being the horseshoe tournament overseer. And much to his chagrin, he enjoyed stamping children's activity cards to receive a free prize. Now, you might know a little more about our Clyde!"

I'm back. I am Trudy Richards. Holiday dinners at the Prestons' were absolutely wonderful. Any and everything you could imagine was served. Thanksgiving had the turkey, dressing, mashed potatoes, and gravy, but also a great green bean dish that had mushroom soup, french fried onions, and cheese in them. There would also be a second potato, like sweet potato or yams, a second vegetable, maybe corn, cranberry sauce, and a wonderful mixed green salad with at least six dressings, some were homemade like blue cheese, and of course, homemade rolls or bread. We were invited so many times; we were treated like family. Ruth always made sure I had plenty of leftovers for at least one more meal. The table was set so very nice with name tags where each of us was to sit. Each one of those had a different flower on them—so cute. They always had company; everyone loved to go there.

I am Alan, Trudy's son, and I am with my mom. I was treated like a son, brother; this was good for me because I was an only child. I loved going over there for many meals because they had much bigger dinners than we had. I also loved to go on vacation with them. They went to so many more different places than my parents. We always went to relatives, and the Prestons went to great places like the ocean. Going over, someone would say, "Alan, where were you yesterday?" Now, tell me how would that make you feel? It made me know that I was loved! My parents absolutely loved me but I felt it more at their home. I think big families are much better. Also, we knew many families and none were like the Prestons. I learned from Mr. Preston how to be a dad, not that my dad was bad; I just got to see him with many kids, and that makes a difference. I also remember Christmases at their place, which are much bigger than ours. It was so much fun to walk in and I did not have to knock. At my house, people had to know to be let in. I would only open the door and see the hundred presents under the tree and around half the living room! I liked that and wanted to have a big family too. That was only one reason I wanted that. When we were on vacations, it was so much fun because sometimes it would be two or four of us that would do something and sometimes it would be all of us. With my parents, it would always be the three of us always doing things together. Life is so very much different in a big family. I also loved having a brother; we shared so very much. It is different sharing with a brother instead of parents. Please learn from the Preston story; your life, like mine, could be so different!

I am Janine, the fifth child. My father, Clyde Elmer Preston, was a good man, a very good man. He was kind, very friendly, very funny, and extremely generous. I loved to watch him interact with others. Daddy always had something to say, something to give away, or better yet, something to trade. That was the best—the trading and the bartering. Nevertheless, if you did not have anything to trade, you always leave our house with a full belly, plenty to drink, and almost always two to three shopping bags of goodies, razors for sure, Listerine, and shampoo.

Daddy was a proud man and rightfully so. He provided very well for his wife and family, and his family stretched to be many a family. I remember Daddy co-signed or loaned money to many members of our huge family, cousins, nieces, nephews, aunts, uncles, children, and friends. If my father could help you out, he certainly would. There were many times when we kids would sleep on cots to make room for others that were in our rooms. My father brought my Aunt Elizabeth, Uncle Walter, and most of their nine children to Rancho Cordova from North Dakota. He helped them with their house and to get my uncle a job. He helped them until they could manage on their own. It was like my parents were "the rock" of the family, and they truly were.

I did not always think so, but Daddy was a very good judge of character. He either liked you or he didn't. He instilled in me that there was not anyone worse than a liar, a cheater, or a thief. "For God's sake, and for your mother's sake too, you better not turn into one of these." Daddy and I had an understanding that the outcome of my actions would always be better if I told him the truth about a situation. I was allowed, however, "not to talk about it," which of course did not go over very well. Those are the times that I wish I had told him the truth from the beginning. It would have been so much easier. Daddy and I talked about almost everything, so it was not any great shock to me when he told me the one thing that will stand out in my mind of the things to remember, and that is, "a prick doesn't have a conscience." Sorry, guys, it seems to be true.

Daddy also so taught me a lot of skills. I think that he was expecting me to be a boy. That's not to say that I was not every bit of a daddy's girl; I was while growing up. He expected me to just as good at something as my male counterparts. I turned out to be a huge tomboy and the best lizard-, crawdad-, snake-, and bug-catching kid there was. To this day, I still have the title. This, however, can change at any time because you see, Clyde Elmer has a great grandson who was given Daddy's name. Clyde Joseph Preston, Brent and Danielle's son, is about as good as I was at his age. The kid is good!

Daddy taught me how to lay concrete, build a fence, and paint and restore houses. He taught me car maintenance, tire and oil change, and checking all the gauges. He taught me how to fish, how to check crabs, smelting, dig for clams, and much more. One time when I was really young, my father had me help him put together a fire engine that I thought was for another little girl. Boy, was I surprised that when we finished putting it together, Daddy handed me the keys. It was an early birthday present and I loved it.

Once when I was a smart-ass teenager, my father made a $10 bet with me. The bet was that he did not believe that anyone with long hair could have or hold a good job. I took the bet; I had to. You see, I knew that Dave, Dad's favorite clerk at Lucky's grocery store, had long hair. My father was surprised to find out that Dave wore a wig. I think he was also surprised that not all longhaired people were bad people. Dad and I taught each other a lot of things, but most of all we learned together what it is like to be family and to love each other unconditionally.

I will always be proud to say that my father was Clyde Elmer Preston, a man who touched many lives.

I am Clyde's sister, Phillis, and it was great growing up with him. He took great care of me and my younger sister and brother. He was a great cook and he taught me how to cook, not my mom. He always made sure I got to school and friends safely. He also made sure that any boyfriend treated me right and he really approved of Tom Donavan, the man I married. Everyone liked my brother Clyde more than the others. He was very smart, very funny, and was so nice to everyone. It seemed that nothing bothered him. I was so sad when he left to go to war. I was only eleven and really wanted my big brother. He had been so very good to me. He was also great to my family after I got married! We all loved it when his family would come to visit us. We all wanted them to stay longer. The kids loved to go horseback riding and we adults love to visit. All was good!

Three Stories About Clyde
from Sooz's Collection

Golfing on Vacation

Clyde was my uncle by way of marriage to my mother's sister, Ruthie. The sisters were very close, and when Clyde passed away in 1985, my dad said of him, "He was my best friend." The Prestons lived in Sacramento and my family had stayed in North Dakota, so when we'd get together, it was special vacation and party time. These were all fun people, so my memories of the Prestons are rich. Not only were the grown-ups a lot of fun but their lively kids numbered six!

Back to Uncle Clyde. Here, I will tell one of my Aunt Ruthie's stories. She had a great sense of humor and the best stories. Life was an adventure for her, and she shared it!

So Ruthie, Clyde, and their youngest son, Billy, age thirteen, were vacationing at Pismo Beach in their fifth wheel with their daughter, Mary, and son-in-law, Clark. One afternoon, while the gals were relaxing in the camper, the three guys (carrying their golf clubs) went out to see what kind of trouble they might find. They came upon a private golf course where they, with Clyde at the helm, made themselves at home. Before long, they were approached by a man of authority who demanded, "Who told you that you could golf here?" Clyde, stumbling over his words, felt compelled to come up with something, so he said, "Well, um, my *wife* did."

Shortly thereafter, Billy arrived back at the camper. His puzzled mother asked him, "Where are Clyde and Clark?" So Billy related the tale, including his dad's faux pas and how they all took off in different directions before the three had to face the consequences of their actions. Ruthie and Mary were a bit horrified and asked him, "They left you *all alone*?" Wide-eyed young Billy answered, "Oh Mother, at a time like that, it's every man for himself."

* Note: This might seem to some like a story about Billy, and of course it is. But for those who knew Clyde, his relationship with his wife, and the empathy he could inspire in his son, it's so Clyde!

The Robes

My mother was a seamstress. She sewed for people all over the county and occasionally beyond. Some of her clients were Catholic priests. Uncle Clyde and Aunt Ruthie happened to be visiting us in North Dakota at the same time Mom was altering some lavish priestly satin robes belonging to Father Niles. Since Clyde hadn't seen them, Ruthie got the brilliant idea that she, Mom, and I should don the robes, one of us at the lead and the other two walking behind in a kind of procession, waving smoking incense burners. So doing just that, we paraded through the living room where Dad and Clyde were having their happy hour.

My Dad chuckled quietly, never too shocked by anything my mom might do. And unflappable Clyde's only comment was "Where'd ya get the incense?"

The House

Mom and I had found an amazing abandoned farmhouse about thirty miles outside of our small North Dakota town. It was in the middle of a sheep pasture and probably hadn't been lived in since the 1950s. It was four floors chock-full of treasures from the past, including its own taxidermy "museum" in the attic. Mom and I loved to explore such houses. It seemed clear to us that no one cared about them or their contents. My Dad did not approve of this practice, but Mom and I just couldn't "keep out."

When Aunt Ruthie and Uncle Clyde were visiting from California, Mom and I described this "best house ever" to Aunt Ruthie. "I'm dying to get in" were her words. So when Clyde and Dad went out for an afternoon of golf, the three of us set off on our adventure. When we got back home, Mom had to admit to Dad where we had been, especially since Ruthie was beside herself with enthusiasm. Typical Dad was mad as hell, and for all the right reasons ("trespassing, robbing"), even though we hadn't taken anything (much). But Uncle Clyde jumped right in and said, "We should rent a truck and go back!"

Dad and Uncle Clyde were the best of friends. It didn't matter how different they were. I think Dad really wanted to be more like him. They're all gone now and I miss them. Clyde, Ruthie, Fred, and Veta, RIP.

We all know that our dad, Clyde Preston, is a unique person, but he was not the only Clyde Preston. One time while visiting Mom and Dad, they told us a story about a young man in Oregon who was looking for his dad. I believe the man was in his early twenties. He was told his biological father was named "Clyde Preston" and somehow he figured out that his dad belonged to the Sacramento Elks Club, so he called Dad's club and asked for the phone number of "Clyde Preston." The club gave the young man the number of "Clyde Preston." He called that number and when Clyde answered, he said something like this: "Hi, Dad . . . I'm your son in Oregon!" After a long pause, Clyde informed the young man that he had not been to Oregon, and the man on the phone was not his son. However, there were two Clydes in the Elks Club and he gave the young man Dad's phone number. The young man called Dad and announced, "Hi, I'm your son. I live in Oregon." Dad's mind was racing and asked the young man exactly where in Oregon he lived. Upon learning the name of the town, Dad heaved a sigh of relief and told him that he was not his father. However, he knew the

"Clyde" Preston who lived in that town and was most likely his real father. Dad then related the story of his elder brother, Earl, who at one time had a family in the San Francisco area and one day decided he had enough. Earl had gone out on the Golden Gate Bridge, took off his fancy shoes, put a "goodbye letter" in his shoes, and climbed up on the rail to jump off. A driver stopped his car and convinced Earl to go with him to Oregon. Several years later, Dad was doing his rounds selling up in Oregon, went into a diner for lunch, and asked the waitress if there were any Prestons in town. She told him about a "Clyde" Preston who worked two stores down in a shoe store. When Dad went to see this Clyde, he found his presumed dead brother. Dad helped his brother get a job in the Sacramento area and gave the help that Earl needed. Dad had a photo from the paper that had a picture of the young man with his real dad, Earl Preston. I know Mom teased Dad about his lost son and I guessed the other Clyde Preston teased Dad also.

CPSIA information can be obtained
at www.ICGtesting.com
Printed in the USA
BVHW081402020719
552485BV00007B/87/P

9 781796 042238